POWER
of THE
SOUL

Also by John Holland

BORN KNOWING: *A Medium's Journey—Accepting and Embracing My Spiritual Gifts*

101 WAYS TO JUMP-START YOUR INTUITION

PSYCHIC NAVIGATOR: *Harnessing Your Inner Guidance*

•:• •:• •:•

Hay House Titles of Related Interest

CALM: *A Proven Four-Step Process Designed Specifically for Women Who Worry,* by Denise Marek

FOUR ACTS OF PERSONAL POWER: *How to Heal Your Past and Create a Positive Future,* by Denise Linn

GET OUT OF YOUR OWN WAY!: *Escape from Mind Traps,* by Tom Rusk, M.D., with Natalie Rusk

THE HARMONY OF HEALTH: *Sound Relaxation for Mind, Body, and Spirit,* by Don Campbell

MIRRORS OF TIME: *Using Regression for Physical, Emotional, and Spiritual Healing,* by Brian L. Weiss, M.D.

MENDING THE PAST AND HEALING THE FUTURE WITH SOUL RETRIEVAL, by Alberto Villoldo, Ph.D.

THE POWER OF INFINITE LOVE & GRATITUDE: *An Evolutionary Journey to Awakening Your Spirit,* by Dr. Darren R. Weissman

REMEMBERING THE FUTURE: *The Path to Recovering Intuition,* by Colette Baron-Reid

REMOVING THE MASKS THAT BIND US, by John Randolph Price

TRUST YOUR VIBES: *Secret Tools for Six-Sensory Living,* by Sonia Choquette

•:• •:• •:•

All of the above are available at your local bookstore,
or may be ordered by visiting:

Hay House USA: **www.hayhouse.com**®
Hay House Australia: **www.hayhouse.com.au**
Hay House UK: **www.hayhouse.co.uk**
Hay House South Africa: **www.hayhouse.co.za**
Hay House India: **www.hayhouseindia.co.in**

POWER OF THE SOUL

INSIDE WISDOM for an OUTSIDE WORLD

John Holland

HAY HOUSE, INC.

Carlsbad, California • New York City
London • Sydney • Johannesburg
Vancouver • Hong Kong • New Delhi

Published and distributed in the United States by: Hay House, Inc.: www.hayhouse.com • *Published and distributed in Australia by:* Hay House Australia Pty. Ltd.: www.hayhouse.com. au • *Published and distributed in the United Kingdom by:* Hay House UK, Ltd.: www.hayhouse. co.uk • *Published and distributed in the Republic of South Africa by:* Hay House SA (Pty), Ltd.: www.hayhouse.co.za • *Distributed in Canada by:* Raincoast: www.raincoast.com • *Published in India by:* Hay House Publishers India: www.hayhouseindia.co.in

Editorial supervision: Jill Kramer • *Design:* Tricia Breidenthal
John Holland's editor: Simon Steel

Library of Congress Cataloging-in-Publication Data

Holland, John.
  Power of the soul : inside wisdom for an outside world / John Holland.
     p. cm.
  ISBN-13: 978-1-4019-1085-3 (hardcover)
  ISBN-13: 978-1-4019-1086-0 (tradepaper) 1. Psychic ability. 2. Soul. 3. Spiritual life.
I. Title.
  BF1031.H627 2007
  131--dc22

                                                                2006024534

Hardcover ISBN: 978-1-4019-1085-3
Tradepaper ISBN: 978-1-4019-1086-0

10 09 08 07   7 6 5 4
1st edition, February 2007
4th edition, October 2007

Printed in the United States of America

To spirit, my guides, family, friends,
colleagues, and students —
all who continue to be my ultimate
teachers in this lifetime.

CONTENTS

❖ ❖ ❖

*Imagine yourself as a luminous
being of energy and light,
because in reality . . . you are.*

— JOHN HOLLAND

INTRODUCTION

Here, a few years into the 21st century, there has been an explosion of interest in spirituality, psychic phenomena, mediumship, metaphysics, and self-help. They're all on the rise and are continually increasing in popularity as people seek meaningful answers to some of life's more obscure questions. I've noticed over the past few years, and even more so today, that individuals from all walks of life are sensing a shift deep within themselves. I believe that this shift can be attributed to a feeling of searching, as if we somehow know that there's something more. It's as if our soul is calling and reaching out to us.

I believe that this happens when our soul urges us to stop looking to the physical world for answers — to stop seeking comfort from physical possessions (such as new cars, toys, and so forth) and start looking within for those long-awaited answers. Our soul is part of us and wants to partner with us in this lifetime. It's going to make every attempt to get our attention in order to assist us, but it's equally essential that we meet it halfway by reaching back.

There's an abundance of evidence that we're no longer receiving the answers we need from the outside world. Attendance is at an all-time high at spiritual workshops and meditation groups, and bookstores are packed with reading material that will ultimately help us *remember*, and *reconnect* with, our true Divine nature.

In this book, you're about to embark on an incredible life-changing journey, which for many might be long overdue — a journey that will ultimately show you, as a soul, just how special and unique you truly are. This work reveals to you that you're so much more than just a physical body . . . you're a spiritual being with unlimited potential.

My own journey has led me from being a student to being a teacher, but I realize that there will always be so much more to learn. I've been a practicing psychic medium and spiritual teacher for more than 17 years. I wrote my first book, *Born Knowing,* to explain the path that I followed and often fought, although I know that I've had guidance from the Divine Source. Two years later, I followed it up with my second book, *Psychic Navigator,* which provides an array of life-changing tools for readers to harness their inner guidance. Today, I'm privileged to teach people my signature workshop, "Learn to Awaken Your Psychic Strengths," which has opened the door for thousands of people, and in return, feeds my soul. I believe that I strive to remain connected with my soul-self; and that my job here on Earth is now to impart as much knowledge, support, love, healing, and direction as I can during my lifetime.

When I felt the stirring in my soul to write another book, I put it out to the Universe and asked to be guided or shown what was needed from me. What could I possibly say to those who are so spiritually hungry that hasn't previously been written in the hundreds of books already on the shelves? Listening to participants at my workshops and lectures offered me a clear consensus of what people are seeking — and here's another interesting shift: A few years ago, it was all about getting a psychic reading or a message from the Other Side; now the questions are centered on how people can be more in tune with their soul and tap into their own intuition. They want to find out how to help themselves enhance or change situations and conditions around them. To put it in the most basic way I know of, people want to stop *sleepwalking* through their lives. I feel that they're ready to push forward through their comfort zone, beyond their natural boundaries. I see it in their eyes all the time . . . it's as if they hope to discover how they can wake up so that they can take a more active role in their own spiritual development and apply this knowledge to their lives.

This was the sign that I needed, so I knew that I had to write this book to show you that, in fact, you already possess *everything* you need. In a way, I intended it to be a sort of alarm clock to wake you up from the inside out. When you write a book, you start off believing that you're doing it for everyone else, but then you soon realize that it's just as much about you as it is about the reader.

This past year of writing has been quite cathartic, as my soul attracted what it needed for its own learning and growth. I had to experience and practice many of the lessons for myself before I could pass them on to you. As a result, I've learned and grown as a person, but more important, as a soul. I believe that each and every one of us is the writer of our own life story, and since it's all about free will and choice, it's up to you to decide how you want your individual story to change and progress. Take your time turning the pages of your life, savor it, and appreciate every moment. Let your soul experience as much as it can along the way. Allow it to help you live life to the fullest with courage and passion so that life doesn't end up "living" you.

In *Power of the Soul,* I want to share my knowledge and personal experiences, as well as some of the inspirational stories from other people who've touched my life. The book is filled with techniques and lessons that I've been taught over the years, many of which will, I hope, benefit you. I've even included some useful material from my other books, because people have told me how much they've enjoyed and benefited from this information, and I feel that some things are worth repeating.

I want to help you manifest and strengthen your body, mind, and soul. I also hope to equip you with some tools to let you break free from your past, showing you how to heal yourself as well as others. I'll reveal how the soul uses intuition and explain the importance of relationships to the soul. You'll even learn about the continuity of life and the journey and immortality of the soul. There are sections that cover synchronicities and how the soul tries to reach out to you to get your attention so that you may listen and heed its guidance.

Your soul is quite wise, and it will always call or attract to itself what it needs to learn in this lifetime. I don't believe in coincidences, and I feel that it's not a random act that you picked up this book at this point in time in your life.

As you read, you'll not only understand, but you'll appreciate, that you're not just human but also a soul — one that's infused with the Divine Source. *Power of the Soul* isn't intended to take anything away from God, the Divine Source . . . it's meant to enhance your connection to It. Above all, I hope that I can teach you to understand and know that this Source loves you unconditionally, running forever through your soul and reaching out in all directions so that you continue to touch and affect each other.

There are no limits or boundaries to where your soul can lead you in this lifetime. As you connect and tap into its power, you'll start to understand yourself on a soul level and become all that you're meant to be — a beautiful extension of God — so that your soul resonates, shines, and most of all . . . illuminates.

CHAPTER ONE

Understanding
the Soul

W hat does the word *soul* truly mean? Have you ever asked yourself the questions *Where is the soul? Does it go on after we die? Does spirituality have anything to do with it?* — and better yet, *How does God fit into all of this?*

Through the ages, scholars as well as all religious and spiritual traditions have contemplated the definition, significance, and nature of the soul. Some people believe that *soul* simply suggests another word for *spirit,* and that they're really one and the same, or that it implies a religious or even a spiritual quality. You may often hear the word *soul* used in today's modern culture referring to a sense of pride in areas such as religion, social customs, food, music, or even dance. I've even heard the word used when expressing a deep-felt emotion — for example: "He put all of his heart and soul into that performance" or "That person has so much soul!" I've been doing my own research on the soul for many years, and I've been amazed by the number of definitions and references there are for one single word, which itself can mean so many different things to so many different people.

Soul *is* consciousness. It's *my* belief that the soul is the true essence of a person. When you look into a mirror and see your reflection, you notice your body, your hair, your eyes, your smile, or even your frown! The reflection looking back at you, the image you see, is just your external shell; it's not who you *really* are. The soul is the person within your body. Your personality can oftentimes be an instrument for your soul to express itself in the outside world, and this plays a significant role in how you relate to others and to yourself. No two souls are ever alike; fortunately, every one of us is unique. It's your soul that determines who you are and what makes you . . . *you.*

Some people ask, "Why should I acknowledge the existence of my soul?" To put it as simply as I can, I'd say, "Because we're spiritual beings in a physical body having human experiences." Therefore, since you're both a physical and spiritual being, you should honor *all* of you. If you go through your days denying yourself the experience of combining these two sides, you're missing out on so much of what life truly has to offer. Why lead a life that's half lived?

Many people who surround themselves with material possessions are under the false impression that doing so will bring happiness, fulfillment, and a sense of purpose to their lives. Even when they acquire these things, they often find themselves asking, "Why do I still feel so empty inside?" People who live spiritually and who work from a soul level realize that there's so much more to this existence than the visible and materialistic physical world. I've noticed that these individuals seem to get the bigger picture, a higher perspective or view, and have both a richer understanding and a deeper meaning with respect to who they are, what they do, and how they conduct their lives. In contrast, if you're the type of person who continues to seek answers from the outside world alone, then I hope that perceiving and working with your soul will confirm that there is true wisdom and guidance that's readily available and can be found within. This phenomenal place of unlimited resources is accessible to each and every one of us, and once you begin to recognize that, you'll start to *feel, see,* and *experience* a world that you never thought possible.

When I decided to write about the remarkable power and abilities of the soul, I wanted to provide you, the reader, with an understanding (based on my research and personal beliefs) of the soul and how it differs from the meaning of the word *spirit.* Throughout this book, I will refer to both concepts.

In ancient writings and references in the Bible, man is described as a triune being, which means that he consists of the three interrelated parts: the body, soul, and spirit. The soul has also been described as an envelope animated by the spirit; and the physical body, in turn, acts as a protective envelope for the soul. When I first heard this explanation, it reminded me of the matryoshka, or Russian nested dolls, placed one inside the other, with their ever-decreasing sizes.

To help you better understand the difference between soul and spirit, here's a simple analogy: Imagine an automobile of your choice. The outside or shell of the car is your physical *body;* the driver is your *soul,* steering the vehicle in different directions and destinations; and the gas that fuels the vehicle is your *spirit.* The Divine force of spirit is what infuses and feeds your soul, pushing you ever forward to strive to be all that you are and all that you could hope to be in this life.

Spirit is the life force, the vital energy that animates us all. It's the spark or the portion of the Divine Source that's in every living thing, and it has a consciousness of its own. In Eastern traditions, the spirit force is known as *chi* in Chinese (or *prana* in Sanskrit), and it's referred to as *ti* or *ki* in Hawaiian. We may be uniquely distinctive and individual souls, but there's a commonality that binds us all together, a spiritual force. The same energy that makes up the stars in the sky — which is the same energy that's coursing through the Universe — is in each and every one of us. As a matter of fact, it was believed in ancient times that each star visible in the sky was the soul of one person. Thus, it was thought that just as the stars shining brightly at night can help guide you through the dark, so too can your soul.

Meeting Your Soul-Self

How well do you know yourself? We're so many different things to so many different people that it's a wonder we know who we really are at all. We conform to what society expects of us. We have a tendency to wear a mask that adapts and changes according to the person, group, or situation we face. These masks come in all shapes, sizes, and forms, including the happy mask, the victim mask, the "I'm in control" mask, the "Nothing is wrong with me" mask, the know-it-all mask, and so on. We adopt so many of these interchangeable masks to fit our every need, yet sometimes we wear one of them so much that we have trouble taking it off! It's almost as if we fear what we'll find underneath if we remove it permanently. Will we even recognize the face staring back? Will we like that person? Do we want to be that person again? We often hide behind these masks to feel safe, which prevents us from showing just who we *really* are.

To live a spiritual and physical life of happiness, serenity, and abundant health — and to experience a loving and successful relationship — it's important to understand and get to know your true essence, your soul. You must begin to go inward to meet your soul, to move through all the layers of what's been built up inside and around you over many years. Once you discover and meet your soul-self, you'll radiate pure light, confidence, courage, strength, and unconditional love for yourself and others. As you live and view your life from your soul's perspective, you'll begin to recognize yourself as a Divine being and gain a deeper appreciation and awareness of the soul essence in others.

I want to tell you a special story that happened a few years ago. It's often said that some people are attracted to light, yet others seem to emanate it. I was privileged to see the luminous brilliance of one man's soul when I was on a whale-watching trip. Ken and Pat, the parents of a very good friend of mine, are from Great Britain and were in the U.S. for a visit. I thought that I'd surprise them by taking them out on a very special boat trip. It was one of those perfect summer days as we drove down to the harbor. It was the first time that Ken and Pat were going to experience being on a whale-watching excursion, and I was excited about the possibility that we'd spot the magnificent humpback whales that frequent the waters off the coast of New England from spring to fall.

As the boat slipped away from the harbor, Ken was clearly eager as he looked overboard, scanning the water with his binoculars. The boat gathered speed and we headed out into the ocean, which was unbelievably calm. It was about an hour and a half later that we saw the first spouts in the distance from a family of whales.

The captain announced that we were going to edge closer to them. He explained, "Male humpback whales sing the longest and most complex songs in the animal kingdom, each one lasting for half an hour or so. They sing to woo females and frighten off rival males, and the songs can be heard underwater hundreds of miles away!"

As the boat came to a stop in the water, everyone got quiet almost out of respect for the whales, which just added to the tension and excitement. You could tell that the animals knew we were there, and it was as though they put on a show for us. Ken's face resembled a child's as he watched in awe while the whales surfaced, twisted onto their backs, and disappeared, their tails the last thing visible before they slipped back into the ocean. As they surfaced again, they started slapping the water as if they were waving to us in unison. Each time they twisted and slapped, everyone let out a gasp.

I glanced over to Ken and was literally stopped in my tracks by what I witnessed. I no longer saw a man in his late 70s; rather, I viewed and experienced him as a soul. There was a light emanating from him, which had the energy and youthfulness of a seven-year-old. I felt the love radiating from his soul, reaching out in all directions . . . it's the most powerful energy in the Universe. I reached out to ask if he was enjoying himself, and as he turned and looked at me, I pretended not to see the tears in his eyes, which reflected the joy and wonderment that he was experiencing. No words were necessary. When you see the Divinity in others, it just reminds you of the same force within yourself. I was blessed that day with a memory that will forever be etched in my soul, as well as in my heart.

I hope that this story demonstrates to you how precious we all are to each other, reinforcing and confirming that your soul — or, in other words, your true inner-self — has always been there for you and always will be, no matter how many times you may have ignored or turned away from it. Your soul communicates with you throughout your entire life, and you've experienced it many times without even realizing it. There are numerous examples: a book you've just read that made you think, the tears when a certain memory surfaced, the love you feel for another person, the movie that struck a chord, a meeting with someone who's unexpectedly changed your life, or the incident that enraged you and prompted you to fight for a cause. If you ever want to see a soul expressing itself, just look at the work of an artist or watch a dancer move to music. Yes, it's true that some people will say these are just human emotions, but feelings stir the energy of the soul.

The more you connect with this part of you, the more you remember your Divine nature. Connecting to your soul can be done in many ways, including meditation, prayer, working on a creative project, journaling, or simply doing something that you love. The following section will assist and encourage you to tap into your inner-self, where you can meet, mingle with, talk to, and listen to your soul . . . it's waiting for you.

Mindfulness of Breathing: A Way Inward

Tuesday nights are very special to me. As often as I can, I join a small group at a Buddhist temple that's hidden away in the woods. Nature seems to cradle this special domed sanctuary safely within her arms: As you step out of your car, the noises from the outside world seem to evaporate and you become aware of the quietness around you.

One particular evening, sitting in the great hall, I was taught a technique that I now practice faithfully and that I want to share with you. I use it often when I meditate in order to reach inside, to connect and be one with my soul. I also practice it when I need to relax, or sometimes when I simply want to fall into a peaceful sleep.

At the temple, a monk in his sacred robes slowly walked in, bowed to the golden statue of Buddha, and rang the gong, which resonated throughout the building. There's something very reas- suring to me when I hear that deep tone echo through the temple. As if by magic, when I follow the sound inwardly, it takes me to a place of peace and ultimate stillness.

The monk instructed us in the practice of the "Mindfulness of Breathing." Of course, you don't have to be a Buddhist or even sit with a group to try out this technique — you may choose to be alone. It's very personal, but I prefer to meditate with others in a spiritual environment. The special energy that comes from the rest of the group seems to enhance the beauty of experiencing oneness. The reason I'm suggesting this technique is to get you to open up your mind, body, and soul consciousness to the power of the breath. The breath can be an amazing tool, and when used properly, it can take you inside yourself, where you can meet your soul halfway.

By practicing this exercise, you'll develop and strengthen the power of mindfulness, which simply means being aware of the breath as a meditative tool. By observing it, you'll be able to enter a state of deeper relaxation while remaining conscious. It's a wonderful place to feel, honor, and acknowledge that you are in fact more than yourself — you are a soul.

Mindfulness is the opposite of *distraction*. It's the ability to maintain an easy sense of focus and attention, and is a way to keep your mind from jumping from thought to thought — just by the simple act of conscious breathing. The more *mindful* you are, the more aware you'll become of yourself and what's going on inside of you, along with what's happening outside and beyond yourself. . . . So let's get on with the exercise.

You'll be using the breath as an object of focus. There's no need to force your concentration by fixing your attention on it or holding it with determination. Throughout the exercise, try to notice how one breath follows another with little or no effort. Let the breath breathe you. When you do this exercise, you'll become more attuned to the rhythm and the inward and outward flow of the breath, as well as to the sensations and feelings that go with it. Practice this technique anytime you wish. I hope that, like me, you'll use it for the rest of your life.

EXERCISE: Mindfulness of Breathing

Make yourself comfortable, preferably by sitting with your feet flat on the floor and your hands relaxed in your lap. For this meditation, you're going to use your nose to inhale as well as exhale. There are four steps to this exercise, and it's important to complete all of them in the right order, since each will assist you in observing and experiencing your breath. At first, practice this breathing meditation for about 20 minutes — or you can extend it longer if you prefer.

So, if you're ready, let's start with **Step 1**. (Remember, each step should take about five minutes.) Close your eyes, relax, and let's begin:

Count your breath to help you connect with it. Just watch your breath come and go with as little effort as possible, as it follows its own natural rhythm. Count at the *end* of each outgoing breath, and count ten breaths in this manner. Then continue doing so for another ten breaths. Keep counting in the same way.

> *Example:*   Breathe in, breathe out, and count one.
> Breathe in, breathe out, and count two . . .
>   and so on, up to ten.
> Then, breathe in, breathe out, and count one . . .
>   and continue counting the same way until
>   you reach ten again.

Let's move on to **Step 2**. Now, I want you to shift so that you're counting just *before* the incoming breath. Although this change is quite subtle, it will create a different emphasis in the way you focus and pay attention to the breath.

> *Example:*   Count one, breathe in, and breathe out.
> Count two, breathe in, breathe out . . .
>   and so on, up to ten.
> Continue in ten-breath cycles.

For **Step 3**, let go of the counting completely, and simply observe the breath come and go with no effort. Enjoy the experience as you become even more aware of the total sensation of breathing. Also, pay attention to those small pauses between the breaths.

For **Step 4**, the final one, lightly focus your attention on the feeling near the tip of your nose and your lips as your breath comes and goes. Try not to strain or force anything at this point. Just practice a relaxed focus on your breath. Become aware of the tranquil energy inside of you, and give yourself a few moments to blend with this force as you become one with it. Feel how far the energy of your soul reaches outward. Sense the love within your heart, the impression of tranquility and peace as you meet and experience yourself as a soul. This is who you are . . . this is your soul stepping forward to meet you halfway. Remember this feeling as you bring yourself back to the present. Please don't worry if your eyes well up with tears — it's quite natural, as your heart, a space that might have felt empty for quite a long time, is being filled. We all go through this when our soul touches us, and through this meditation exercise, you'll experience the unlimited power of this part of you.

This particular breathing meditation is a wonderful way to spend some time each day not *doing anything,* but *just being.* The minutes that you spend observing your breath will not only restore you physically, emotionally, and mentally, but will instill in you a sense of peace and alignment with your soul. The breath has its own way of constantly reminding you to remain in the moment . . . the here and now. By working with it, you'll learn to let go of the past, stop worrying about what will be, and reduce the stresses and strains of everyday life. You'll start to focus on today, right now — this very moment. It's during these periods of quietness that you're likely to hear the whispers of your soul more easily and discover where the true power of spirit resides.

To end this section, here's one more little exercise you can do if you don't have time for the longer breathing meditation: When you want to experience the sensation of being with your soul, or when you feel that you need to slow the pace down because life gets chaotic, simply close your eyes, put your hands over your heart, breathe deeply, and say to yourself, *Find your center.* By doing so, you'll connect with your soul, where you'll discover that you're able to let go and gently relax into the present.

Charting the Course

When you acknowledge and follow your soul, you'll embark on a journey to a special place deep inside, and you'll discover all the tools you need to start *thinking* and *feeling* from within. It's a location where you'll not only feel safe to talk to your soul, but you'll be able to listen and follow its wisdom. Over time, you'll begin to view your life, the world, and everything around you through more spiritual eyes. You'll become aware of and develop an extraordinary new understanding, one of increased compassion, forgiveness, acceptance, and healing. In this quiet place, you'll establish your own unique relationship with the Divine Source and see how It molds Itself to the patterns of your life. During these times, you'll experience and receive many insights, so I recommend that you keep a journal close by to capture your spiritual progress and record the patterns weaving in and around your life. Find or make a journal that is *special* for you.

When I write in my journal, it's as though I somehow step off the busy merry-go-round for a moment — the world stops for a few seconds as I pause for a breath. It's my time to reflect as I attempt to make sense of and interpret my feelings and appreciate what my soul or life is trying to show me. By recording your thoughts, you're consciously getting them out of your head and onto paper. The sheer action of writing them down provides a clearer view of what's happening within you. You may start noticing a pattern of events and situations in your life, and as they become more evident, you'll see with increased clarity just what you can do to enhance or stop them.

For many years, I've kept my own journals, and from time to time for no apparent reason, I look back with pride and joy on the progress in my life, occasionally laughing at some of the mistakes I've made. I can see how I've grown, and I appreciate the significance of some of the important lessons that I needed to encounter along the way. My journal has helped me learn from past experiences and has become an invaluable resource to assist me in navigating through the complex maze of life. So if you haven't already started to, I suggest that you keep your own Soul Journal and commit your thoughts and feelings to paper as you record your spiritual journey. Please don't worry if you're not a competent writer or if your grammar is a bit hit-and-miss! Just remember, this is your journal — it's totally private, and you have no one to impress, so you can be completely honest and free.

As you grow as a soul, you'll learn new lessons, gain new memories, become inspired, and hear and tell stories. Prayers will be answered, and people will enter your life as you raise your consciousness and vibration. New goals and affirmations will be added as your aspirations develop, meditations will reveal incredible insights, intuitive flashes and impressions will show up with increased clarity and regularity, and events will guide and change your life. All these things remind you of who you are — and better yet, they'll show you the potential for how far you can go.

A personal journal becomes your best friend as you record these new insights. As an author, I've used some of the material from my journals as a reference for the books I've written. I hope that you build your own journal so that when you look back in years to come, you'll see just how far you've progressed.

The spiritual discipline of journaling is meant to be so much more than just a record of events . . . it's a way to relish time with yourself, and it will help you connect with your soul on a deeper level. Try to look upon it as a form of meditative conversation with your inner-self: It's your time to ask your soul questions and then — through all of the synchronicities, intuitive flashes, insights, and impressions — see how the answers appear.

Spiritual Journaling Tips

1. It's best to try to write in your journal around the same time every day, and preferably in the same area. I find the early hours of dawn quite inspiring, but you should write when it's right for you.

2. Take your journal on your travels so that you can record information about the people, places, and experiences you encounter.

3. You don't have to show your writing to anyone if you don't want to. This is for you and your soul, a safe place to share yourself with the Divine Source.

4. There's nothing too small or too insignificant for your Soul Journal; it all counts.

5. Record as many happy memories as you can — that way when you're feeling down or low or need inspiration, you'll have them to look at.

Finally, you may be asking what else you can record in your Soul Journal. Here are just a few more ideas:

• Jot down how your day went. Did you learn or discover something new about yourself or someone else? Include any fresh insights that you want to share about yourself.

• Begin to record your personal goals and desires.

• Write down affirmations that really inspired you, or make up your own.

• Include any current prayers, or keep a record of the ones that were answered.

• Record inspirational words of advice that someone might have given you, your nightly dreams, and meditative insights.

• Make a note of new discoveries as you read back on what you've written in the past.

• Start a list of what you're grateful for in your life.

• Add any symbols, drawings, or images that you feel are coming through inspiration.

- Keep track of synchronicities, along with psychic and intuitive impressions.

Journaling isn't meant to be a chore; it's really just a vehicle to cultivate a good working relationship with your soul. As you complete your entries, you'll feel spirit moving within you and guiding you. You'll notice how you and your soul start integrating as you become one. Throughout this process, the *real* you will begin to emerge. Your thoughts will take on greater clarity, and you'll gain access to some of those unanswered questions as you reach deeper within yourself. Try not to overanalyze everything . . . just get out of your own way and be honest with the Divine Source, as well as with yourself.

Soul Purpose

At one time or another, we all have asked ourselves, *Who am I? Why am I here?* and better yet, *Where am I going, and how on earth do I get there?* These questions are quite common and are usually followed by the statement *There's got to be more than this!*

Sound familiar? I believe that our soul purpose is: (1) *to be all that we can be,* and (2) *to live our lives in alignment with our highest good.* We should acknowledge, impact, and help each other as much as we can with our unique gifts, talents, and abilities. As a soul, you've chosen this time to learn specific lessons and perform certain tasks. Your particular talents and abilities are meant to help you be happy, enjoy life, achieve your true potential as a spiritual being, and become all that you can be — a beautiful extension of God, the Divine Source.

We all have important work to do while we're here on this earth, and we've chosen to incarnate in physical form to fulfill our soul purpose. Sometimes people can get confused if they think that their career, goals, or tasks are their *soul purpose.* But it isn't about becoming the president of a company, winning awards, or saving the world. It's more about affecting people and the planet in a positive way. My soul purpose isn't so much related to becoming a well-known psychic medium, author, or teacher (abilities and talents that were provided for me to use); rather, it's about influencing and having a positive effect on others. I believe that this is *my* gift to give, and my purpose is to perfect myself as a soul in being all that I can be during my time here.

Years ago, I remember doing an amazing exercise from a book that revealed how to talk and interact with one's angels and guides. I thought it was the perfect time to ask why I was so conscious of my intuitive psychic abilities. As a boy, I was the one who was "different." I was highly sensitive and aware of things that other people didn't appear to sense or even notice. No, it wasn't easy growing up with these abilities and being labeled "strange," "weird," or "freak"! I made it my mission: I had to know *why* was I born this way.

The exercise in the book explained how to quiet one's mind and expand one's consciousness enough to converse with one's angels and guides. I followed the instructions to the letter: I lit a candle and set about quieting my thoughts, which I did by just staring at the flame until the mind chatter subsided. I stopped thinking about all the things I had to do later and just concentrated on the moment. After a few minutes, I relaxed and could feel myself slipping into a meditative state.

When I felt ready, not really knowing what to expect, I asked the question in my mind: *What is the purpose of my being so psychic?* Without even the slightest pause, a stream of words started downloading into my mind like someone had opened the floodgate. It was an amazing experience, and I certainly wasn't expecting to hear what I heard: "Your psychic abilities are like a schoolteacher in front of a blackboard with a pointer, and they should be used as a tool in their own right. Just as a teacher uses a pointer to emphasize words on the board, your abilities are meant to aim people in the right direction. They're not the *whole* of you, but a small part of you. They help steer people toward the discovery of their own spirituality." And as suddenly as it had started, the flow of words was cut off. I felt a creeping awareness spread through my body as I started to understand why I was born with an elevated level of perception. At that moment, I realized that my abilities were meant to help people achieve their own soul purpose of being all that they can be.

As I grew up, I ran as fast as I could away from these gifts, but no matter what happened, I was always brought back to the stark reality that I would be using them, whether I liked it or not, for the rest of my life. It was about that time that I noticed how like-minded souls were constantly attracted to me, whether I was sharing some wisdom or offering some type of direction in their lives.

Over the years, my soul purpose and gifts have grown, evolved, and even changed — and so will yours as you continue on your journey. I've been blessed to witness some beautiful souls who've had such a profound effect on those around them. Each is unique in how he or she uses the special talent or gift that he or she was born with to reach out and touch others, spreading joy through comedy, inspiring people to write and compose music, or building confidence and self-esteem. No matter *how* they're reaching out or giving back, the point is that they're sharing themselves with others unconditionally. I encountered one such soul who has a wonderful capacity to inspire others when I took a drawing class some years ago.

Eric, an experienced art teacher, is a living example of someone acting out his soul purpose. He works with students, helping them explore and develop their artistic talents and spread creativity. He has an extraordinary way of motivating his students to tap into their own soul. In doing so, he encourages them to create inspirational art that has quite a profound effect on other people. He compels and urges them to dig deep within themselves and connect with their own creative inner beauty. It's as much fun just to watch him teach as it is to be taught *by* him. When you stand back and observe him, you can see the vitality of his soul beaming all around him, and it creates a ripple effect with the people he touches. The power of spirit is strongly flowing through him, and there are no barriers or boundaries to block the energy coursing through his being . . . he's in the flow. I believe that this happens because he's doing what he's supposed to be doing — that is, helping aspiring artists become all that they can be by using his gift of teaching, creativity, and art. Eric is truly living and following his soul purpose of being all that *he* can be, and he's affecting humanity with his incredible talent in a positive way.

There's a purpose for you, too — and as much as you try to ignore its calling, you're constantly drawn back to the fact that you're yearning for more out of life and have the need to understand who you *really* are. There's no better way to experience your soul, heal yourself, and have a stronger connection with God than by living your soul purpose. It's when you tap in at this level that you'll cultivate a better sense of self. When you're not living your true soul purpose, you may suffer from a lack of self-esteem and feelings of stagnation and disinterest, or you might experience times when a sense of absolute tiredness overwhelms you. People who don't embrace their purpose will often take jobs for the safety and security of a regular paycheck. I'm not saying that this is wrong, as I totally understand that we're spiritual beings inhabiting a physical, material world. Nevertheless, when you begin acting out your soul purpose of being all that you can be, you start living your life to its full potential. This is when the power of spirit flows through you easily and you become energized and excited about life.

As I've said earlier, we're all born with special gifts, talents, and abilities. Yes, even you! But right now you may be saying, "How do I know what they are, and how can I find them?" Let me help you, showing you an easy exercise to get you on your way to living your soul purpose. It will aid you in identifying your innate endowments as you embark on your own journey of being all that you can be.

EXERCISE: Discovering Your Soul's Gifts

Get out a piece of paper, and draw a line down the middle. Now, at the top of the left-hand column, write the name of a person you admire. Take a moment to think about this so that it's someone you really do look up to. Close your eyes, and as you imagine that individual in front of you, ask yourself what you admire most about him or her. Open your eyes, and make a list under the person's name. Is it his or her strength, courage, professionalism, or ability to laugh? Write down anything and everything that you've come to marvel at about the person.

Once you've completed the list, go to the right-hand column of the paper and think of someone who you know admires *you!* At the top, list what that person respects about you based on things that he or she has said in the past. Is it your humor, compassion, kindness, or generosity? Now compare the two lists: Notice that some of the qualities you wrote in the left-hand column are attributes that also appear in the right-hand one. I believe that what you admire and see in others is actually a soul reflection of what's inside of you. This is a great starting point for learning how to notice and work with your own distinctive gifts and talents.

Once you discover your own special abilities, you'll be able to apply them in your everyday life. Whether you're at work or at home, they can be used to help you attain your true calling. There's also a bonus: When you follow your soul purpose, things seem to come to you a little easier, or you may find yourself in the right place at the right time to gain the opportunity to achieve a particular goal. The first step is living and doing what you love, and the second is to start *now!* Don't try to run before you can walk, however, as I would encourage you to take small steps toward your goal — at least you're moving in the right direction. Having observed many people who are doing what they love, I can almost see the energy of excitement, joy, and enthusiasm that emanates from them. I describe it by saying that their soul has become "positively infused." It's as if I'm seeing them lit up from the inside out.

I try to practice and live my life according to Paramhansa Yogananda, who said: "Life is to be lived. If you live abundantly and use all your talents and energies to the limit every day, you'll develop ever-greater power and understanding of your full potential as a soul. There's no end to the life, love, power, and wisdom that could be yours if you start using what you have."

Here's another exercise to assist you in living your soul purpose. Use your journal or a piece of paper, and answer the following questions, taking as long as you need. (Come on, don't read on or skip these questions. Grab that pen and try this!)

1. What am I passionate about?

2. What did I enjoy doing as a child?

3. What did I imagine at a young age that I wanted to be when I grew up?

4. Have other people noticed or commented on what I'm good at?

5. Is there a hobby that I take pleasure in?

6. How could I make a career out of what I love doing?

7. What am I engaged in when time seems to just fly by?

8. What do I enjoy reading in my spare time?

9. What kind of people would I like to be around me?

10. What can I do right now to take a step closer to doing what I love?

When you immerse yourself in the conscious stream of your purpose, you'll feel your passions pulsing through you. You'll become aware of a sense of vitality, along with the love within yourself, your life, and all that you do. It's almost akin to feeling like a kid again. Have you ever watched children at play? I believe that they're still living from the place they left not that long ago — the world of spirit. They're carefree and full of energy. It's as if time has no meaning for them and they're not yet trapped in this physical world. Then as the years go on, life, society, expectations, and other people's opinions and influences begin to pile on the layers over the simplicity and freshness of childhood, and eventually they forget that they're a soul and why they've come here.

Therefore, I urge you to make the time to go back and investigate where you originated and how you got to be here. Are there incidents in your life that might have been showing you, or leading you to use, your soul's gifts and abilities? When you discover what these are, do something as soon as you can to start living your soul purpose of being all that you can be. Begin by asking yourself the ten questions I've just listed to help you uncover your talents. You'll start to identify and find the answers that have been there all along. It may not always be easy, and there could be times when it's frustrating, but don't give up. By taking the first step and beginning to look inside yourself toward your soul — the *real* you — you'll start to form a uniquely personal, lifelong partnership that will help you with the most wondrous of journeys: the one that we call life.

CHAPTER TWO

Acknowledging
the Source

Life has its own unique way of showing you miracles every day. However, with so much information in this world vying for your attention, messages or subtle hints from the Divine Source can often be missed. (When I talk about "Source," I mean God, the Universe, or a Higher Consciousness — call It what you will.) People feel and experience Source in any number of ways, be it through meditation, dreams, synchronistic events, or even an act as simple as giving gratitude. Jan, a new friend who worked with me in Arizona, told me that when Source is trying to get her attention, she receives goose bumps, but I loved it when she said that she prefers to call them "God bumps."

The Divine Source will always try to work with you to form a partnership, but it's up to you to welcome and greet It in order to secure a good connection. In the following sections, I want to teach you a few ways in which It manifests and works in your life so that you can recognize, acknowledge, and act on It.

Synchronicities

Synchronicities and so-called coincidences are clear signs that the Divine Source is knocking on your door. Sometimes it might be a soft tap — or for those occasions when you're not paying attention, it could be a loud bang! Source working through synchronicity can manifest in some unique ways. I have my own definition and refer to them as my *Divine nudges*.

Have you heard the same phrase or saying from more than one person in a day? Do identical numbers keep showing up in your life? Has someone mentioned the very name you were just thinking of? Have you met an individual out of the blue who seemed to answer a question that you were just pondering? These are all simply signs for you to pause, be open, pay attention — and most important, acknowledge that the Source is sending you a message.

I heard a story once about a man who was having a hard time switching careers, and all the unanswered questions were clearly causing him a lot of stress. He was offered a new position and wasn't sure if he wanted to leave the security of his existing job, where he'd been for years. One day as he was driving to work in a state of indecisiveness, he found himself asking the questions that we all put ourselves through at such times: *Should I take the new job? Will I be happy? Am I doing the right thing?* At that precise moment — just as he was churning these questions over and over — he saw a bus drive by, and for some reason, he read the billboard on the side of it: It was a Nike advertisement with the slogan "Just Do It."

These are *not* merely coincidences! I don't believe that there are accidents in this intelligent Universe. It's times like these that you should ask yourself, *What am I supposed to be learning or doing right now?* I feel that when these synchronistic events happen, the *inner* workings of your soul are showing up in your *outer* physical world.

In my first book, *Born Knowing,* I talked about a time in my life when I was really tired — emotionally, mentally, and psychically. I was holding down two jobs: working my normal 9-to-5 day job and then in the evenings seeing private clients for psychic readings or to work as a spirit messenger. I couldn't keep up the pace and prayed for an answer. The pressing questions that bugged me were typically: *Could I work as a full-time psychic medium? Would I be able to support myself? Do I really want to have a career as a psychic?*

As you can imagine, I did a lot of soul-searching during that time, but out of the blue an extraordinary synchronistic event happened. It was to become a turning point in my life, and it occurred at rush hour on the crowded train during my regular commute home! The subway station was the usual zoo as people pushed and shoved to get on the trains. It had been a particularly busy day at my job, too. I knew that I had to get my second wind because as soon as I got home, I had four clients booked, so it would be a late evening.

That night, although the train was packed, I was lucky and got a seat. As we lurched out of the station, I glanced to my left and noticed that the seat next to me was still empty. I shrugged and was about to go back to the book I was reading when I looked up to see an elderly nun in her full habit standing in front of me. I didn't notice where she came from — she was just there.

"Hello, young man," she greeted me. "You have a nice face. Is the seat next to you taken?"

"No, Sister, please go right ahead," I said, sliding over a few inches to make more room for her. As the train gathered speed, I could feel her watching me while I was trying to read. I turned to her and noticed the bluest, kindest eyes I'd ever seen. In fact, she seemed to be looking right inside of me. "My name is Sister Agnes, but most people call me 'Aggie' for short," she said.

"Hi, I'm John," I replied. Clearly, she was determined to talk the whole way home, so I put down my book and decided to politely listen.

"Can you guess what I do for a living?" she asked.

"Well, let me see . . . um . . . you're a schoolteacher?" I said with a smile.

Sister Aggie returned the grin and continued, "No, I help those who are ill and live in hospices or in the hospital. I help them get ready to die and cross over. Many people call me a 'Counselor for God.'"

My mouth dropped open, and all I could say in my characteristic Boston accent was an excited: "Sistah! Did you ever sit in the right seat! You get them before they go, and I get them after! . . . I'm a medium." In my world, she rated as a "special" person due to the nature of her work, so I asked her how she got through the tough times.

"My job is to give others love and compassion. I'm sure you can relate to that, John. The work you're doing is equally important, but I know you're good at it," she said, looking gently into my eyes.

How does she know how good I am? I wondered. *She has no idea who I am!*

"You're giving people 'Memory Days,'" she continued as though she were probing my mind. I was intrigued and fascinated by this woman, for her words resonated with me.

"What do mean by that, Sister?" I inquired.

"John, some days come and some days go," she replied quickly. "People don't realize that every day is a new beginning and a chance to start over. There are days that people remember forever, while there are others that simply slip away into their yesterdays. You never know when you're giving someone a Memory Day. It can be an act of kindness, a trip to the country, or something as simple as helping an elderly woman with her groceries. People remember these special days for the rest of their lives."

She paused to let the significance of her words sink in. "John, we take these memories with us when we pass," she went on, "and I do believe that we review our lives, with all our faults and accomplishments. Why not have the best memories by our side and try to give good ones to whomever we can?"

As she spoke, I knew that we were both on the same spiritual wavelength. She continued, "All we can do is our best. That's why you and I are here — so we can do the best possible job with the time we're given." She stopped speaking as I suddenly realized that we'd pulled into Harvard Square Station. She'd timed her speech perfectly, as if she knew how long I'd be sitting on the train. I wished her the very best and said a heartfelt good-bye.

Sister Aggie stood up and flashed me her biggest smile. "Bless you, John. Keep up the faith," she said with such tenderness in her voice.

"You, too, Sister," I replied, glancing down for only a split second. When I looked up, she was gone. Sure, it was crowded in the station, but I didn't even see her blend into the crowd. I knew that I couldn't explain her presence but that I'd never forget her, because she'd left me with my very own "Memory Day."

I know that our meeting was destined to be, as I needed to hear what Sister Aggie had to say at that precise time in my life. I realized that I wouldn't be working two jobs for much longer because I had to follow my true calling. Sister Aggie is what my colleague Cheryl Richardson refers to in her book *The Unmistakable Touch of Grace* as a "spiritual change agent." These are people who unexpectedly step into your life through synchronicity and provide the answer to a question you were contemplating. Their influence can put you on a new path, bring to you an alternative understanding, or even change your life altogether.

In Chapter 1, I used the analogy of seeing yourself as a car when you're thinking about the difference between soul and spirit. Synchronicities act as signposts or mile markers guiding and directing you — or even helping you align with your personal growth. Notice when you're being sent such signals, people, patterns, books, articles, and the like. I think of them as special little gifts that help steer you on your path toward your goals and assist you in following your soul's guidance.

Tips on Tapping Into and Working with Synchronicities

- The more you notice and pay attention to meaningful synchronistic events and coincidences, the more they will multiply in your life.

- Notice when you run into people unexpectedly. Really listen to what's being said in the conversation and the hidden message that could be there for you.

- If there's a certain problem in your life, try to let it go and turn it over to synchronicity. What you're saying to the Divine Source is: "Okay, show me! Let me be *aware* and *act* when the answer or guidance is being presented to me."

- Work with your journal and your intuition to become even more conscious when Source is knocking on your door.

- Believe that it's possible. A positive attitude enhances the experience, just as a negative one will shut it down.

Dream Talk

Your subconscious constantly and subtly speaks through your dreams, which is just one of the many ways that your soul can reach out and communicate with you. We all dream to some extent every night, even if we're not able to recall doing so the next morning. We remember some of our dreams with great clarity of interpretation, some we struggle to figure out, and there are others that just slip away as soon as the day starts. If you're not working in partnership with your dreams, then you're missing out on a great resource for helpful advice, guidance, and direction. Over the years, I've taught myself to acknowledge and listen to my dreams. For example, I know that if I dream I'm immersed in water up to my chest, then it's often symptomatic of the onset of bronchitis, so it's a sign for me to take extra care and up the dose of vitamin C. In other words, I *acknowledge* and *act* on the warning signs being given to me.

A friend of mine named Adrianne called me recently to tell me about an unforgettable dream she'd had that she found really enlightening. She was animated over the phone as she explained it to me: "John, in my dream I saw myself walking into my bathroom, and I noticed that there were hundreds of ants crawling over my best terry-cloth towels!"

It's important to stress that Adrianne is quite an aware person, and she knew that her dream would be trying to tell her something. She continued with her story: "So I began to describe the dream in my Dream Journal, which I keep beside my bed. It's so strange, John. I kept focusing on two words as I was writing. They just stood out." I was intrigued and asked her to tell me the words.

"They were *ants* and *terry* — they literally jumped out of the page at me." Adrianne explained how it immediately dawned on her that she hadn't heard from her Aunt Terry in a while. She'd learned to interpret dreams from years of practice, so as she stared at the two words *ants* and *terry* together, her aunt popped into her mind.

This vivid dream motivated her to call her mother and ask about her aunt. Her mom said that she thought it was strange that she hadn't heard from her sister recently. Of course, that was enough to set off the warning bells. Her mother got on the phone and called around to the rest of the family, who likewise hadn't heard from Aunt Terry. Everyone was by now so concerned that they called Aunt Terry's neighbor across the street, who looked out the window and said that she could see that Terry's car was still in the driveway. The neighbor ran across the street and rang the bell, but there was no answer.

The family called the police, who arrived within minutes and found Aunt Terry on her bedroom floor, paralyzed by a stroke that she'd suffered two days earlier — she was unable to move. Thankfully, there's a happy end to this story, as she was rushed to the hospital for medical treatment and eventually recovered from her stroke. Had Adrianne failed to acknowledge and act upon her dream, however, Aunt Terry's story would have a sad ending.

When you tap into the power of your dreams, they can provide an unlimited resource for you. Most people don't know that you can often acquire the answers you're looking for by a process called *dream incubation.* In other words, it's possible to program your dreams to help you work out problems or issues that you may be having at a certain time. I highly recommend creating your own personal Dream Journal. If you have a major issue to resolve and you've tried other methods, you could look to your dreams for help.

Here's a useful tip: Before you go to bed, write down the concern in your Dream Journal. It's a bit like submitting your "incubation request." Read it a few times to yourself before you drift off to sleep so that it remains fresh in your subconscious, allowing Source to give you guidance. Try to keep the question or issue as short as possible, preferably down to one sentence. For instance, you might write: "What's the next move for me in my career?" or "How can I improve my relationship?" or even, "What's going on with my body at this time?" It helps to wake up gently, so I hope that you don't have an alarm clock that jolts you awake! When you wake up, write down in your journal everything that you received in your dream that stands out — symbols, feelings, emotions, and even the colors — *before* your feet touch the floor, because by the time you get back from the bathroom, the dream may have slipped away.

You may not recollect anything or feel as though you didn't

dream at all, but don't give up. Try it for a few nights as you get used to programming yourself to dream, and condition yourself to start remembering. Ask the same question for several nights, and record in your journal anything and everything you receive, even if it doesn't make sense. Although it may seem like a puzzle, the pieces will eventually fit together, and you'll see the message of guidance materialize from the fragments. When this happens for the first time, you'll ask yourself how you didn't see it before, since it will appear so obvious . . . that's the beauty of dreams.

Keep in mind that dreams are formed in the subconscious, and they can be quite symbolic. One symbol's meaning for you can often represent something totally different to another person. Analyze the image you receive, as it's subject to your own personal interpretation. If you don't understand it, then pause and ask yourself, *What does this symbol mean to me?* I found it helpful to look at some books on symbolism. That way, such information can be deposited in your mind for future reference. Anything that's been stored in your subconscious then becomes part of your personal data bank that your soul can use later on for dream work or intuitive information.

It's unlikely that you're going to get a clear yes or no to your question. Sometimes your dreams are your mind's way of working through information that's stored during the day — it can be a sort of brain download or mind dump. Even when dreams don't appear to make any sense, it's still worth writing down any- and everything, no matter how stupid it might seem at the time, for there could still be a small message hidden within the seemingly muddled information. As you learn to work with your dreams, you'll recognize the patterns and symbols and be able to interpret how they're trying to get your attention and talk to you.

Here's another quick example from one of my students, who was curious about whether to accept a new job or not. She wrote in her journal, asking: "Is taking this position for my highest good?" That night in her dream, she saw herself walking down a path. It got darker and darker and started raining and thundering, and lightning filled the sky. Well, you can guess how she interpreted the dream — she decided not to take the position. She found out a few weeks later that the job description would have changed to include a much heavier workload. In addition, she knew some of the staff there, and a woman she didn't get along with got promoted during all the restructuring and, ironically, would have become her new boss!

I encourage you to start reading and studying as much as you can as you begin working with your dreams. They're a resource that's readily available to you, and the more you use this soul ability, the more you'll benefit from its guidance and messages. Enjoy dreaming!

Circle of Gratitude

Life is one big continuous circle of giving and receiving energy. As a soul, you're an energetic being composed of an intelligent Source of spiritual energy that guides you on your path toward happiness, prosperity, and well-being. While you should pray for these things and more, it's just as important to stop and give thanks for what you've achieved and acquired. When you're in a state of thankfulness, you actually acknowledge and honor the spirit of your soul — the Divine Source.

No matter what your circumstances are at any one time, there's always something to be grateful for. You might have heard the story of the person who complained about the pain in his legs, until he saw someone with no feet. . . . Let me share another poignant story of a woman I met during one of my lectures.

Before I initiate the link with those on the Other Side, I often open up the floor for questions about anything from psychic development to a dream to some unexplained experience. This particular lecture was at the end of an Alaska cruise, and I remember the day clearly. We'd been up early to witness the spectacular turquoise blue streaked glacier at the top of a fjord, and the ship was now sailing in calm waters down the sound. The lecture theater was packed, and as I paused for questions, there was the usual sea of arms waving for my attention. One woman raised her hand, staring at me with a sheer intensity in her eyes. The microphone had barely been passed to her before she started speaking: "John, can you tell me why I was given away as a child and separated from my ten siblings?" Everyone turned to look at her.

It took me a moment for her question to sink in. I didn't offer up an immediate psychic answer, as I felt that I had to ask her how her life had turned out thus far. When I inquired about this, she practically shouted back, "My life is a total mess!"

I peered out into the audience to look at her closely, wondering how an attractive woman who appeared to be in her early 40s could feel this way. "Aren't you on a cruise ship in one of the most beautiful places in the world?" I asked.

"Yes," she replied.

I continued, "So, how's your health?"

"Fine," she said.

I asked if she was happily married. She kept nodding in answer to each of my questions. "Who's that beautiful child sleeping on your lap?" I asked.

"My daughter," she responded.

I then asked, "Is she healthy?"

"Very healthy," she said.

I finished up by asking her if she owned her own home — she did. "So how does this translate into a mess?" I asked her quizzically. I pointed out that she needed to stop and take a long, hard look at all the good things in her life and be grateful for what she'd been blessed with. I concluded by telling her that I believe every day that you step out of bed and your foot touches the floor, you're doing okay.

I glanced at the clock and realized that I had to move on. I didn't get a chance to ask her about the conditions under which she was brought up, but I was trying to show her how much she really had so that she could let go of the past and live and enjoy her life with thankfulness. I know it's often hard to be thankful if you're ill, down-and-out, hurting, or even depressed. Somehow when you acknowledge and have gratitude for the blessings you do have, an energy shift happens in your soul, and a sense of lightness can be felt, as though a weight has been lifted.

Be thankful for who and what's in your life, instead of complaining about what you don't have. If you focus on gratitude, you'll attract prosperity and abundance. When I say "prosperity," I'm not just referring to financial riches, but also to less tangible things such as love, friends, kindness, health, compassion, and the like. There are various types of prosperity and abundance. Just saying "Thank you" and holding those words inside where they can resonate with your soul will help the connections and good intentions of others to stream into your life and create affirmative experiences. Equally, it's all right to thank yourself. If you've done something positive for *you,* then pat yourself on the back and say, "I thank me." You deserve it!

Appreciate all the abundance and goodness that's around you. Be grateful for your health, your children, sunny days, your garden, family, best friends, or even the person who lets you jump ahead in line at the bank! The more joy you begin to notice and appreciate, the easier it becomes for you to experience more happiness, abundance, prosperity, and most important — love.

Ways of Showing Gratitude

Most of us have heard of the expression "It's in giving that we truly receive." One way to keep the wheel of giving and receiving primed and the flow of abundance streaming from the Source into your life is to practice the "Law of Tithing." *Tithing* simply means "to make a contribution." In ancient religious practices, it signified that you would give a tenth of your income to your church, but it has now spread to different areas of people's lives. I find it wonderful that we're not only tithing religious and spiritual organizations, charities, or other groups, but we're also tithing each other. Helping those around you is what living from your soul is all about. I'm a very strong believer in tithing.

Just as it's important to give, you have to be ready to receive. Many of us have no problem being *givers,* but when it's time to *receive,* some of us struggle. There has to be a flow with respect to both aspects — giving and receiving — for tithing to work successfully.

A number of years ago when I was living alone and trying to make ends meet with barely enough money to get by, I came home one day to find an envelope under my door. It was addressed to me and was from a dear friend. Inside was a letter in which my friend explained how she'd come into a little extra money, and knowing that I could use some, she was giving me a portion of it. I stood there and cried, wondering if she knew how much that meant to me at that time, not just from a financial perspective, but on an emotional, spiritual level. To me, it showed that people still cared — that we can reach out and touch each other's lives. Before she'd signed the note, she explained how she was practicing the act of tithing and had thought of me first.

Many years later, my friend was down on *her* luck. She'd moved to a new city and was looking for a job. I returned the gesture and gave her back what she'd given me, and then some. When she left me that gift years ago, she didn't do it as a loan or expect to get anything back . . . she gave it as an act of kindness, gratitude, and love. I'll never forget it. Materially, she may have given me money, but in reality at that time, she offered me hope.

When you tithe something to others, they don't need to know who it's from; it's the act of giving that's important. We tithe all the time when we contribute to charities, or even when we volunteer our time — which is a form of the same thing: the act of giving back.

By giving back, you're acknowledging and honoring the Divine Source, and in doing so, you're keeping the energy of the "giving-and-receiving circle" open and flowing. When you focus on having an *attitude of gratitude,* you're really sharing so that everyone benefits.

Here are just a few ways you can express gratitude:

- Saying prayers of thanks
- Giving love unconditionally
- Offering blessings for what you do have
- Acknowledging a good deed from your neighbor
- Donating your time to your chosen charity
- Giving food or spare change to a homeless person
- Saying a kind word to a stranger
- Sending a card to someone who could use encouragement
- Smiling at others

Believe in the Impossible

Have you ever noticed how some people seem to have all the luck? Do you wonder if there's a secret or magic formula? The force that works through your soul — determining what's possible or impossible, the difference between success and failure, and above all, who we are — is the power of your belief. Some people have faith in a higher power than themselves. There are those who trust in love and abundance, while sadly others believe that they're alone and are only meant to survive. Some just walk aimlessly upon this planet, accepting whatever comes their way.

It's not about luck; it's about how and why you're attracting such conditions in your life. By consciously believing and knowing that spirit is running through you and that you're meant to lead a happy, abundant existence, you'll experience life the way you were intended to live it — as a soul. In the following sections, I want to take you through some different techniques for affirming what you want and the absolute power of words, as well as feeling and believing that you can have the things you desire in this life. This will help show you that the *impossible* can indeed become the *possible.*

If you're anything like me, then you're likely to have read dozens of books or heard speakers talk about the power of positive thought, visualization techniques, and life-changing affirmations and how they can benefit your life by teaching you to focus on what you want. It's a system that works, but you can't just see something in your mind's eye and expect it to materialize into your life that easily. It has to be a partnership with the Universe, in that you must take an active role and more important, *believe* that this system, which has worked for millions of others, can work for you.

A woman I knew was having a particularly bad day, and I remember her saying to me, "John, I can't stand it: You seem to have been born with a lucky horseshoe! You always get what you want effortlessly!"

I felt the sting of envy and an all-too-familiar negative energy coming from her, so for once I turned to her and retorted: "Are you kidding me? It's not about luck . . . it's how I've lived my life and always will." She'd been saddled with the same mind-set for years. She believed that the world was a tough, hard place and everyone was out to screw you over — her words, not mine! She believed that her world wouldn't and couldn't ever give her what she wanted. It's a tragic mind-set when it gets so firmly ingrained in one's consciousness and energy. This is the way she'd always thought, so it's not difficult to see how her inner thoughts created her own outer reality, which in her case was her own hell. Her story is a classic example of someone who hasn't tried to connect on a soul level, who's stuck in a recurring cycle of self-afflicted pain, disappointment, and lack of personal fulfillment. Life truly does follow thought.

This story also reminds me of a time in my teenage years when a friend said something that I remember to this day: "John, nice guys finish last." Even now, I refuse to believe that statement. The majority of people live their lives by the rules and conditions that were imposed upon them by their parents, society, the media, the government, their religion, and other influential people. Such rules, behavioral patterns, and conditions are instilled in us while we're young and impressionable. My family's all-time favorite saying while I was growing up was: "We *never* have any luck!" So, I grew up believing that luck didn't come my way. Fortunately for me, I learned to reprogram that thought!

Here are a few more sayings that you're sure to remember:

- "Life is tough."
- "Be happy with what you have."
- "Money doesn't grow on trees."
- "There's only so much that can go around."
- "Take what you can get, and feel lucky that you got it."
- "You can have that when you win the lottery."
- "That's nothing but a pipe dream."
- "Who do you think you are?"
- "It's a dog-eat-dog world."
- "Life wasn't meant to be easy."
- "You're just a dreamer."

And let's not forget the ever-popular saying that can be found on bumper stickers, T-shirts, notebooks, and so forth: "Life sucks, and then you die"!

Now, don't get me wrong — I don't want you to think that I'm constantly wearing rose-colored glasses. I too had a hard life in my earlier years and still have difficult challenges and situations to deal with (and I'm sure that more will be put in front of me in the future), but it's a matter of choice . . . it's how we view our lives, how we choose to live them, and how we go about healing ourselves. Life's greatest gift to us is the power of free will, which is what separates us from the animal kingdom.

I grew up in an abusive, alcoholic home in a tough, impoverished neighborhood where being a child meant living with constant fear and anxiety, wondering what disaster would happen next. I quickly adopted a defense mechanism that resulted in a breakdown of trust and belief. The incessant fights, drinking, and abuse meant that I led a life of shame and guilt, believing that I was never smart enough or good enough. I eventually conditioned myself to believe that this was as good as it was going to get.

Over the years and through self-reflection, personal therapy, and reading a vast amount of spiritual material, I realized that my entire life was about choice. I had the choice of how I wanted to live and how I could potentially heal myself — and it was this realization that saved me. As I tapped into the depths of my soul, I knew that there had to be more happiness, and that I didn't have to suffer or become a victim of my upbringing. It was time to take off the shackles of the past. This became a lifelong mission. *I had to do the work.*

We may not always be responsible for the hand that's dealt us, but it's up to us how we *play* that hand. I believe that some things are meant to happen, and that you chose these conditions before your soul was incarnated into your present body. However, it's your free will to decide what to do in that situation when it happens. I can now look back and see that through my upbringing and all the hurt that went with it, I have a far better understanding of pain and compassion when I'm helping my clients cope with their loss of a loved one. I now believe that I needed to experience this to be able to do the work I was meant to do.

Your spiritual, emotional, and psychological well-being; your present and future relationships; and your work and career can all be affected by your past conditioning. When certain issues remain omnipresent in your life and you want a chance to deal with them, you may need to take a critical look at your own belief system. It could be time to perform a retrospective on yourself, as well as on the people and world around you. With some of the more stubborn issues, it's perfectly okay to seek the aid and counsel of experienced professionals to help you overcome these obstinate hang-ups. It's then and only then, as you work together, that you'll be able to move on and learn new ways of living. You don't have to do it alone.

What I'm trying to say here is that to manifest the life you truly want, there may be old beliefs or past conditioning that need to be sorted out first. Once these legacies are dismantled and discarded, you'll be able to benefit from following the methods for positive thinking, including visualization techniques and life-changing affirmations. You'll start to feel a deeper and more profound inner sense of happiness, and life will afford you more opportunities to achieve what you want. The Divine Source that's working through your soul right now even as you're reading this book wants to help, but the big question is: "Will you let It help, and are you willing to take the necessary steps?"

You've no doubt heard the expression "God helps those who help themselves." I don't live my life believing that I know everything, but I *do* know what's worked for others as well as myself. I hope that you'll benefit from my learning and experiences so that you understand and realize that as a soul, you do have the power to trust, believe, and manifest the very best into your existence!

Life Follows Thought

You are what you think. Most people don't realize how powerful thoughts are, and that each one has its own unique energy signature. You're a magnetic energy being, so when you have a thought, it's immediately lodged in your magnetic field — more commonly known as your *aura*. When that thought remains there for any length of time, it's often radiated out and absorbed into the Universe. It's easy to imagine what's likely to happen to people who constantly fear that they're going to be robbed. They're consciously thinking about it, dwelling on it, feeding their precious energy into it — and as a result, they send that stream of fear-based thought out into the Universe. It's as if they're holding up a sign with a giant arrow above their heads saying: "Hey, come rob me!" . . . so that's exactly what happens. Then you hear them say, "I knew this was going to happen!" It doesn't take rocket science to see that we *attract* what we *think*.

I remember moving to Los Angeles and borrowing a friend's car. I was nervous since it was so new, and even though I'd driven it before, I dreaded anything happening to it. Well, of course I did have a small accident . . . not once, but three different times! I know what you're saying: "Well, why did his friend keep letting him use it?" She was a good friend and trusted me. In reality, the accidents weren't my fault — it was more a case of the other drivers hitting me! Nevertheless, I believe I worried so much about damaging her new car that I drew the accidents to myself. Eventually, I told myself, *John, you're a perfectly good driver. Trust and know that you and the car are always safe.* I acknowledged that although it wasn't my car, we did have insurance and I was a responsible driver. The accidents stopped occurring.

So, we've already established that some of our current thinking can be traced back to a legacy of old programming. Imagine this as a cassette tape that keeps playing the same thoughts repeatedly. It's time to replace it with new, more uplifting, life-affirming thoughts.

I know someone who starts every week off in the same way: Even before she gets out of bed, she says, "Monday — another long week ahead!" It's as though she's just programmed the week for herself, so you can well imagine that by Friday she's exhausted.

Every year this same woman and her family go on a week's vacation to one of the most spectacular lake resorts in New England. The water is surrounded by thousands of acres of lush green forest, and kids can be heard laughing and adults enjoying themselves. She waits *all* year for this break from her hectic lifestyle.

When she arrives on the very first day, she unpacks, and then as she sits down, she lets out a long sigh, stating: "Only six days left . . ." She doesn't even enjoy being in the moment, thinking instead about how much time remains! It's as if her conscious thought is already packing up to leave — not a great start to a vacation.

You've heard the saying "Like attracts like" — well, it's really more about *frequency attracting the same frequency.* As I've said, everything is made up of energy, and that includes you and me. Since we're energy, it's probable that we'll tune in to and attract the same frequency that we resonate: If we're afraid, we'll draw fear to ourselves; if we're kind, we'll attract compassion; if we're grateful, we'll attract prosperity. As we think, we begin to feel; as we feel, we vibrate; and as we vibrate, we start to attract . . . in other words, we'll attract exactly what we're resonating.

You should be careful of your thoughts (positive or negative), for if you continually think about something, it's possible that you'll ultimately attract it, as though you're a giant magnet. When you carry out any of the following exercises, it's important that you're not thinking negatively, saying: "Oh well, I'll read this stuff and maybe try it, but I'm not even really sure if I believe it." If you approach it from that perspective, you're still in a mode of thinking with thoughts of disbelief as opposed to those of trust and belief. You'll be forever fighting the process, and as a result, you'll block the flow of attracting what you really want.

Try to become more aware in the future of how and what you're thinking. A great thing to do every once in a while is to ask yourself, *How are my thoughts today?* You might be very surprised that they reflect exactly how your day is going. I encourage you to study, investigate, and read more about the power of thought. One fantastic book on the subject is *Ask and It Is Given* by Esther and Jerry Hicks. One of the most important things to remember in this life is the power of thought and the law of attraction. It's worth remembering that you're *always* certain to find what you're thinking, or looking for.

Seeing Is Believing — the Power of Visualization

The power of the human mind and the capabilities of our soul have always fascinated me. When I finally made the decision to write my first book, *Born Knowing,* I was somewhat nervous, as I'd never written one before. I'd known for a while that it was time, but somehow I had to get into a mind-set of just doing it. I spoke with numerous other authors, read books, and even took a class on the best way to write. Everyone has their own writing style. Through my spiritual awareness and all the reading I'd done, I knew that I had to begin a process of visualizing the finished book.

Visualization is simply a technique whereby you use your imagination to assist you in creating what you want in this life. I remember that day I sat there, quieted my mind, and went into a meditation to picture my very first book on the shelf at my local bookstore. I imagined myself walking into the store and looking for it. As my eyes roamed up and down the shelves, I finally saw it in its entirety: its size, the color, the cover design with its powerful image, and even the spine of the book displaying the title with my name. I saw myself pick it up, running my fingers through the pages. I used all of my senses, and I could feel the joy and happiness well up inside me as I let my emotions fill my soul. It's one thing to just visualize something, and quite another to sense the emotion that you'd feel, as if you were looking at it in the here and now.

Another example of how I use the positive effects of visualization was the time when my publisher asked me to join three other authors on a speaking tour of Australia. I accepted the opportunity without so much as a second thought. Almost immediately, though, nagging worries started to creep in about presenting in another country. I'd never been there before, and the culture is so different. My mind went into overdrive: *What would the people be like? Would they like me?*

Once again I knew that I had to get into a mind-set based on trusting and believing that I could do it. I visualized myself onstage in front of 2,000 people in Sydney. I pictured myself giving my speech and delivering spirit messages from the Other Side. I saw the audience members with their smiling faces as they intently listened to every word, and I imagined the messages flowing beautifully. I felt the joy of the day and ended the visualization with 2,000 people applauding. I *visualized* and *felt* what it would be like as if it were happening right then. Sure enough, when I finally arrived in Australia, the night was a great success and turned out just as I'd visualized and felt that it would.

Do you even know what you want? Some people will go from psychic to psychic hoping that they will be told something positive or wonderful about their future. However, in reality, the way it works is that yes, a psychic may see something that's not in your realm of consciousness at the time, but you can help yourself if you have some idea of what you want. I'll use the analogy of a bouncing ball, where the ball represents an idea or a specific thought. Working on a psychic level, I follow where the ball is going to land or what direction it will take, but you have to at least start bouncing it! So, before you begin visualizing, you must be able to create a picture of what you desire. I've met so many people who are still unclear about what they actually want, and some don't even know where to start. If this resonates with you, or sounds like you or someone you know, let me try to help.

The best place to start is by letting go of what you *don't* want. If you really can't figure out what you want to do, be, or accomplish, then make a list of people, situations, emotions, and habits that aren't for your highest good. You should be ready and willing to let go of them. So if you are, get out your journal and write at the top of the page: "I *am* letting go of _____." You may add to the list, change it, or even delete it — whatever you want. This is a lifelong process, one that will change and evolve with you. It's a good idea to include a positive affirmation at the end. Here's one of my favorites: "I now release these things from my life for my highest good, and I bless them all. Let go — let God."

Here's one more step to help you figure out what you want: Make a list of all your wishes, dreams, and such — or in other words, what you *really,* really want. Have fun as you create this list, and give yourself the freedom to imagine anything. Write it all down, even if it sounds a little crazy or outrageous . . . it's your own list, just for you. Don't worry about what other people would do or would want for you. This is your soul, your spirit, and your life.

By tapping into all your senses, imagine and write down what the perfect life and job would look and feel like, what you want in a relationship, your dream house, and the ideal location to live. Cover every aspect of your life — nothing is too big or small to write down. Keep thinking of these things throughout the day, and look at them every time you open your journal so that this list starts to integrate into your life as well as your soul. What you're doing is starting to expand your imagination and consciousness, and you're giving your soul a chance to grow and assist you in magnetizing it in the present.

EXERCISE: Visualization

For this exercise, it's best to start slowly until you get the hang of it. If I tell you to "visualize" and you're not getting a clear mental picture, don't worry, as it may take a few attempts. Impressions will start to form as you use your imagination by thinking or even just by feeling. Reflect on an area in your life that you want to work on. Is it a relationship, your health, or maybe a job-related issue? This is a great exercise to follow the previous one about your dreams and wishes. Remember that if you're calm, your imagination will have a chance to flow freely; if you're tense from work or something else, it's going to be harder to relax and get the most from this exercise. . . . So, let's start.

Begin to see, create, imagine, and feel the desired positive outcome you want from the situation or issue that you're going to work on. Picture *every* possible detail that you can: the colors, the scene, the people involved — everything you can imagine and think of. Put your visualization in the present tense as if it's actually happening right now.

Okay, now bring in the emotion that goes with the picture. It's a bit like turning up the volume on your television set . . . you'll have the complete experience. Feel the joy, sense of completion, and happiness in what you're seeing — really, really, really feel it. By *visualizing* the scene, coupled with the emotions that you're feeling, you'll find that this can be a great partnership for manifesting what you truly want and deserve.

The Power of Affirmations

Words have the power to inspire, heal, and transform. Just as they can have a positive effect, they can also be hurtful, especially when directed at ourselves. Do you really want to know how someone's life is going or why it is the way it is? If so, it's important to actually listen to the words the person uses. I believe that you *are* the embodiment of your words. For example, if people are constantly talking about misery and despair, then it's most likely that their lives are a reflection of what they're saying. We all know people like this — it can even be draining to be in their company. You come away feeling exhausted, since they're really inadvertently sapping your precious energy, whether you realize it or not.

Affirmations can be a wonderfully complementary life tool. They are statements asserting the existence or the truth of something. To *affirm* simply means to "make firm." Every word you speak or think is in itself an affirmation. Try writing your own and combining them with the previous exercises to achieve your desires and wishes.

Earlier I explained that my family had a rather unique mantra during my childhood, namely: "We *never* have any luck!" I grew up believing this and set my expectations accordingly. Of course, that's not the sort of affirmation I'm suggesting here, and even though it wasn't exactly a positive one, it was an affirmation nonetheless.

If children are told often enough that they're dumb, useless, or stupid, then those kids will eventually live lives that reflect this belief. In some cases, this can have damaging long-term effects, and I've met many people through my work who suffer to this day from the effects of such negative affirmations. The sad part of these stories is when these individuals adopt the characteristics of those negative affirmations for themselves. When you hear people saying unfavorable things about themselves, they don't seem to realize that just by continually thinking and voicing them, they can manifest negative personality traits. I'm sure that you've heard people assert: "*I am* a loser," "*I am* so stupid," or "*I am* trouble." The use of the very words *I am* is very powerful, as it encompasses your *whole* being, everything that you are. Equally, these can be magic words if you just learn to watch the other ones you combine with them and understand the proper way affirmations should work and the power that they hold.

Affirmation can be used in all areas of your life. To apply them properly and effectively, I've listed a few pointers to start you on your way to affirming the life you want and deserve:

- Always use the first person when stating positive affirmations. For example: "I *am* healthy," "I *am* calm and balanced," "I *am* beautiful," and "I *am* now following my soul's guidance." These phrases are also great: "I *attract*," "I *choose*," and "I *have*."

- When using affirmations, always remember that they're meant to be expressed in the present tense, in the *here and now*. For example, they should not be used like this: "I will have a good relationship someday." By saying it that way, you're signaling to the Universe that it's not important right *now* to have a relationship, but rather, sometime in the future. This is how the idea should be stated: "I *now* attract the perfect relationship into my life."

- Repeat affirmations frequently. Speak or write out your affirmations 10 to 15 times in a row, once in the morning and again in the evening. You can't expect to say them just once and instill any power in them. The more often you say and *believe* them, the more power you're giving them, and the better chance of your manifesting them.

- Be specific. If you have a particular need, then the more detailed and precise you can be, the better the results. If you're affirming a new relationship, list the qualities that you want. For example: "I *am* worthy of love and of attracting the perfect partner for my highest good." If you say: "I attract a relationship," then it's likely that you'll get one, but it may not be exactly what you're looking for. If you want money, then be specific and say: "Abundance is all around me, and I *now* attract [a specific amount] to me quickly."

- Combine your affirmations with your visualizations for an even more positive effect. As you do so, try to see yourself totally immersed in the desire of your outcome.

- Read inspirational books and quotes that encourage and motivate you.

- Change your affirmations after they've been manifested.

- Experiment, and enjoy yourself when making up your own affirmations.

Here are a few examples from my earlier books:

I trust my intuition and myself.
I am a beautiful expression of life.
I now notice when my inner voice is speaking to me.
I now choose to bring positive energy into my day, as well as my life.
I attract all that I need in my life that is for my highest good.
I am strong, balanced, and here in the now.
I am love.

Try writing your affirmations in your journal. Have fun: You may prefer to write them in large type or make them different colors. Stick them as Post-it notes on your computer, your bathroom mirror, or wherever you can see them. Say them as often as you can so that you have positive boosts throughout the day. As you continue to work with the techniques I've outlined, you'll start seeing the inner workings of your soul and spirit reach out to help you achieve all your wants and desires in your outside world. I wrote this chapter in the hopes of getting you to a point where you can believe that having what you want is in fact possible, acknowledging that the spirit force that runs through your soul wants to bring it to you.

If You Can
Think it — See It — Feel It — Say It — and Believe It,
You Can
Become It!

CHAPTER THREE

The Unfoldment
of Your Soul Senses

Each and every one of us possesses the spiritual ability to become consciously aware of the workings of our soul's sensitivity. In other words, we have the natural capacity to tap into our intuitive psychic abilities. One of my favorite statements, which I often say at my lectures, is: "We all came from God, and I don't think a Divine intelligence would let us come here without a little help. The gift of intuition is our connection to the Divine." Although it's something that's given to each and every soul, it's important to remember that we're responsible for developing it ourselves. The word *psychic* is from the Greek *psychikos,* meaning "of the soul." By definition, this signifies that as spiritual beings, we're able to access, receive, and transmit information that reaches beyond our physical body and our innate five senses.

Opening the door to your natural intuitive powers is an exciting, enlightening, and life-changing experience. I've received thousands of letters and e-mails from past students who've written to tell me that since they started working on their all-too-often-dormant abilities, they feel as if their soul is more consciously *alive* and *awake,* as though they're no longer sleepwalking through life. Using the soul sense of intuition is quite natural; and you can learn to recognize, practice, and trust it. By doing so, it becomes a wonderful resource for guidance, transformation, and self-empowerment that you can call upon and share for the rest of your life.

To live an intuitive life, you must *believe* and *know* that you're equipped with all the tools you need. As a spiritual being, you possess unlimited abilities, so it would be wise to acknowledge the potential that's waiting to be awakened; hence, my use of the term *dormant abilities.* The tools that help direct you to your inner guidance are your soul senses — or as I refer to them in my book *Psychic Navigator,* your "psychic strengths." In sum, I'm talking about your inner feelings: *inner knowing* (clairsentience); *inner vision* (clairvoyance); and last, *inner hearing* (clairaudience). As you sharpen and hone these senses, you'll learn how to work with the subtle energetic field (the aura) surrounding everything and everyone, as well as how to use the energy centers (chakras) of the body.

As you start to identify your strongest ability, you'll find that it will open the door to all sorts of experiences. It's as though your soul is guiding you: Your consciousness will expand, and you'll become aware of things that may be buried in the past that you wouldn't normally sense or even recognize. Knowing how to use these abilities will awaken other spiritual gifts and create a heightened awareness of the experience of your soul's journey, bringing you joy, abundance, vibrant health, and life meaning.

(*Note:* Some information in this chapter is taken from my second book, *Psychic Navigator,* which is an excellent resource and companion to this chapter. A more in-depth description of chakras and auras can be found there.)

Intuition: Language of the Soul

At one time or another, we've all had some intuitive experience in our lives. Most of us know what *intuition* means. How many times have we heard someone say, "I've got a hunch that . . ." or "My instincts are telling me to . . ." or "I have a strong gut feeling that . . ." These are all forms of intuition. It's those gentle nudges that frequently just come out of the blue, the ones that we so often ignore or try to wave off as being simply our imagination — only to find out later were correct.

We're all *born* with this ability. It's one of the ways that our soul constantly tries to speak to us, and it's as much your birthright as anybody else's. This natural soul ability isn't purely limited to transcended masters or to people who have devoted a lifetime to studying and practicing meditation. It's not about fortune-telling, crystal balls, or predicting the future. To be intuitive or psychic isn't just something we possess . . . it's more a way of being. It's the language and navigator of the soul, as well as the path to the Divine wisdom within.

We're all born aware, with a deep sense of inner knowing. It's one of the greatest gifts we possess, keeping us connected to our higher selves, the Universe, and the Divine spirit. We're all equipped with an intricate and highly tuned inner guidance system, which we can regularly tap into using our intuitive abilities. Receiving psychic information is all about *energy*. Everything is made up of energy — people, places, and even objects store it — so we can receive and read information by means of our intuitive senses.

Being intuitive is similar to the way a television works: We all know that we can't actually see TV signals beaming through the airways, yet we're aware that they're being transmitted. Our TV sets receive these signals, and they're decoded to form a picture on our screens. The same rule applies when it comes to intuitive energy: We receive information constantly through our psychic senses, and the result, once this data is descrambled, is an impression or feeling that we didn't perceive through our usual physical senses. Now you'll understand why I love the words written by Yogananda: "We are electrical beings with intelligence." As we learn to recognize when our intuition is speaking to us, we hone our skills in deciphering the signals that push us forward to follow our soul's guidance.

Your intuition is actually speaking to you always, but most of the time you may not even be aware of it. I'd like you to take a break for a moment and ask yourself the following questions:

- Have you ever thought of someone you haven't heard from in a while, and out of the blue you receive a surprise phone call or suddenly bump into him or her on the street?

- Have you ever had a hunch that you didn't follow, only to regret it later because it turned out to be correct?

- Do you know on the spot if you like or dislike someone?

- Have you ever been certain of the outcome of a situation or event before it happened?

- Have you ever simply guessed a person's occupation, as opposed to allowing the conscious interpretation of how they look or speak, or their mannerisms, affect your opinion?

- Do you have vivid or prophetic dreams?

- Do coincidences and synchronicities keep appearing in your life?

If you answered yes to some of these questions, it shows that you're already aware of your intuition. It's important to realize that these are just a few examples of what being intuitive is all about. As I've said, most of the time we don't acknowledge this power when it's trying to get our attention because we simply don't trust our inner guidance without facts or logic to validate it. For many of us, we still look upon it as something totally mysterious or even ethereal.

Mysteries can be intriguing, but when it comes to working with your soul sensitivity, you need to understand and learn the mechanics of how it functions. Once you do, it will no longer remain an unknown factor in your life. You can harness this power, and with some dedicated mental training, you'll be able to reap the rewards all-around, since it can become an unlimited resource for wisdom and guidance to assist you in intuitively navigating your way through life. Developing your intuitive abilities requires that you make a commitment to yourself — a commitment to understanding and learning how to live in partnership with your own inner guidance.

A reporter once asked me, "John, with all the negativity that exists around the world, why would I *want* to be intuitively sensitive and pick up on these things?"

I nodded in recognition of such a thoughtful question and replied, "I totally understand where you're coming from, but don't you see that by choosing not to learn and accept that we're all sensitive beings, capable of living with our soul's higher awareness, we're choosing to shut off all the good and beauty that can be felt within the world and each other? We are, and always will be, connected to everyone and everything."

A few weeks later, I was teaching one of my regular workshops on developing your intuition and psychic strengths, and I noticed that the reporter had registered and was sitting right there at the front. I guess I wasn't too surprised!

There are numerous benefits to tapping into your inner awareness, but it's important to remember that it's not just about predictions or finding easy answers to problems. Here are just a few of the rewards of developing your intuitive abilities.

Wouldn't you like to . . .

. . . improve your relationships?
. . . enhance your creative ability?
. . . make the most of your career?
. . . receive intuitive guidance on important decisions?
. . . connect to your loved ones who have passed on?
. . . enhance your physical abilities?
. . . feel more connected to nature and the Universe?
. . . notice more synchronicities in your life?
. . . be more guided on your soul's journey?

You can benefit from *all* of these things and more by using and strengthening your intuitive psychic ability. However, one aspect that most people have an issue with is *trust*. Have faith in yourself, and believe that you're entitled to live intuitively and psychically — to see yourself and the world in a way you never thought possible. Let yourself experiment and play like a child when it comes to your abilities. You're born with a wonderful capacity to play; you had these gifts once, and unbelievably, they never left. I encourage you to think back, reach out, and recapture them.

Preparing Yourself to Begin

Congratulations on making the decision to become who you *really* are. Let's take the first steps in revealing that you're truly more than this physical body — that you're a spiritual being with unlimited potential.

Now that we've established some basic facts about intuition, let's move on to explore and discover your soul's senses and their full potential.

You'll very likely develop your intuition in your own way and in your own time. Don't rush, as there is no right or wrong here. Take all the time you need — after all, it's taken years to become disconnected from your natural intuitive abilities, so finding your way back isn't going to happen overnight. . . . Are you ready to begin?

First, find an area that you can set aside just for you! This room or dedicated space is going to be your place for meditation and studying, and for practicing all the different exercises throughout the book. Most important, it should be a setting where you're not going to be disturbed when you need to retreat for your quiet time. So shut off the computer (the e-mail can wait), and unplug the phone, as you want to establish an atmosphere of total peace.

Try to make this special place uncluttered. It helps for it to be in a well-ventilated area or for there to be a window nearby so that you can let in fresh air to renew the energy. Beyond that, a comfortable chair and a small table are really all that's required, although you might like to have fresh flowers around for added energy. Keep the lighting low . . . you might even burn a votive candle or some incense. It's also helpful to play some soft music, but know that these aren't necessities, just suggestions.

In my meditation room, I have three colored drawings of my guides for inspiration, along with some mementos of spiritual leaders whom I'm connected to — and, of course, my special comfortable chair. The room is painted in soft blues to create a tranquil atmosphere.

Some people decide to set up a personal altar with their favorite photos and crystals. By creating your own special area and only using it for your quiet time, meditation, and personal development, you'll slowly start to infuse the space with positive psychic energy; and it will take on a feeling of its own, which should be one of warmth and peace.

To start off, I find that it's best to meditate at the same time every day so that you can look forward to your special time with yourself and your soul. In doing so, you're training your mind and honoring that commitment. Through continued practice, it gets steadily easier to meditate and develop your inner guidance.

Earlier I stressed the importance of keeping a Soul Journal during your development. I highly recommend that you keep it handy in your special area — remember that psychic and intuitive thoughts can happen anytime, anywhere. Your journal will become a valuable resource in the future as you look back on your progress. It will show you where you were right or wrong and can often become a teaching manual in itself. I have journals that go back years, where I've recorded hunches, impressions, and exercises, as well as my dreams. As I leaf through pages and pages of my handwriting, it's easy to see how my abilities have developed and strengthened over time.

Please don't get hung up on whether you were right or wrong. Making the effort is the factor that's of greatest value, as you discover how your intuition receives information. Once again, it's important to recall that everyone receives and works with their psychic abilities in their own way, and you should never try to emulate someone else. Experiment to see and feel what works for you, and trust that your soul will guide you to what's right for it.

When working with your journal and your intuitive soul senses, make sure that you record your entries with a time and date mark in order to see your progress when you look back days, months, and years later. Here are a few ideas of what you may want to put in your Soul Journal:

- Write down when you feel an unexpected thought or impression coming into your mind that seems to be outside of your day-to-day routine, even if you feel that you're making it up.

- Record the coincidences and synchronicities that seem to continually run through your life.

- Jot down the same numbers that keep showing up in your life, whether you see them on license plates, on clocks, as phone numbers, or what have you.

- Write down your dreams or any images and emotions that you remember from your sleep.

- Draw any pictures or symbols that come into your mind, but try not to edit what you're receiving.

Setting up your special area and keeping a journal during the process of understanding and developing your soul senses will in itself help your consciousness expand, since you'll be beginning to make an effort to work with and get to know your own inner guidance system. This will lead to a gradual awakening as you start to notice how you're working together with your intuition and your mind in trusting and interpreting the language of your soul.

Into the Stillness

To enable us to unfold and tap into our own soul senses, we all need to practice some form of meditation. For some of us, this activity conjures up images of a guru in robes chanting from the top of a mountain, or a monk sitting in quiet solitude within a sacred temple, surrounded by curls of incense smoke hanging in the air. Others believe that meditation is as simple as closing one's eyes and going into a trance, or that at the most basic level, we only need to let our mind go totally blank in order to enter a meditative state. It's not as easy as that. What *is* more achievable and realistic is training yourself to become more aware of your thoughts as they come into your mind and go out again, a bit like flowing water. Soon these same thoughts will lose their power to influence your conscious mind.

Meditation is, in fact, a state of being in which the active mind slows down enough for you to become aware of a place where the mental chatter is silenced. As you slip into this quiet space, you become increasingly *aware* of the subtle shifting energies within you. Much healing can be done when you're deep in meditation and you surrender your physical body to the power of your soul. To develop your psychic/intuitive guidance system, it's essential that you learn to enter, and feel comfortable with, the silence within.

Meditation is a vital part of your personal development. It's simply not enough to read about it — you have to just do it! It's also possible to enter into a state of meditation where you consciously focus your mind on a single point. Some people find it helpful to use mandalas (those beautiful symbols that draw you in), while others visualize images such as a flower, a lovely landscape scene, or a spiritual guide. I also know people who prefer to continuously chant using a single word or sound.

There are many ways to meditate, but whatever method you choose, with solid practice and commitment you'll steadily train your mind to become calm and still. This will foster a sense of well-being that can have tangible benefits in all areas of your life. If you believe that you can't meditate, it's quite probable that you've already done so without even realizing it. For example, when artists are absorbed in their work, they can lose themselves totally in their own creativity . . . minutes become hours. You'll often hear someone say, "I just *zoned out.*" Have you ever had that sensation of time just slipping by without your being aware of it? What's really happening is that you most likely entered into a state of meditation.

We live in a world where so many of us strive to earn more, get better jobs, and buy newer cars along with all the other material things that we believe we need to feel good. This is all fair and well, but it's not the ultimate answer. It's my belief that it's just as important to continually feed our souls. When we're constantly reaching outward to achieve more and more, it's easy to slip further away from the spark of our life force, and our soul may wander off its original track. While we're all born *connected* to the Divine Source, we have a tendency to pull away from what was once natural.

It's reasonable to assume that when we become disconnected from spirit, the Source that once nourished us will be replaced with another source or substitute. In other words, the connection gets forged with food, alcohol, nicotine, codependency, or even work (hence, the term *workaholic*). Many of us spend our lives trying to fill the void that was created when the link was broken.

People are finding it harder to obtain answers from the outside material world, so they're starting to look for resolution from within. When your external existence becomes so hectic, so stressful, that your anxiety starts to overwhelm you, then maybe it's time to stop and ask, *When was the last time I checked in with myself?*

In this fast-paced world, obtaining peace of mind and serenity can be quite a difficult challenge. If we're going to survive, then we must learn to pull back from the stresses and strains of daily life and make time to seek out that inner place of silence, calmness, and peace. Meditation can do that for us. It also produces many health improvements, which I call the "extra benefit."

For instance, the sense of relaxation and calmness that results can enhance your immune system, reduce your blood pressure, and be an invaluable tool for healing your body. Meditating can increase your physical energy, along with your overall well-being. I also find that it's a great way for *me* to look at a problem or situation instead of being *in* it. It's a chance to stand back, view the issue through new eyes and with renewed appreciation, and see where the changes can be made for a healthier or more beneficial outcome.

Now here's the reality check: You may have the best intentions of starting your meditation practice, but life will throw up all the hurdles it can to stop you. That's when you have to make an extra effort to devote the necessary time. To get into the mindset, I suggest that you start by meditating at the same time daily — whenever works best for your routine. Personally, I prefer the morning before I start work; that way, I approach the day calm, centered, and ready to take on whatever comes with a sense of awareness, clarity, and vitality.

Even when life continues to present barriers that prevent you from meditating, don't give up — keep at it for at least seven days. Hopefully, once you've settled into a routine, you'll continue meditating for the rest of your life and wonder why you waited so long to take it up. Start with 15 minutes each day using some of the exercises in this chapter. Soon you'll learn to increase the length of your meditation, and ultimately, you'll look forward to that special time with yourself and your soul.

During these early stages of learning to meditate, you'll notice that your mind will continue to chatter or even wander off, allowing those external influences to creep in. That's perfectly normal in the beginning. Over time, your thoughts will slow down, the chatter will diminish, and you'll start to have a sense of clarity and focus. When your mind is calm and without internal noise, it will become easier to find that place of absolute stillness where psychic and intuitive information flows freely.

Relaxing the Body and Mind

If you choose to become more aware of your soul's inner guidance, you must first learn to relax the body as well as the mind. When your physical self is in a state of calmness, your mind will become still, allowing a sense of total relaxation and clarity to take over. Meditation will help you integrate your body, mind, and soul so that you feel centered and grounded, promoting a state of balance. You'll feel more capable of dealing with your busy schedule; and over time, meditation will alleviate some of the tensions that you may be holding inside your body. Once these strains are released, other associated minor ailments could disappear as well.

The body and the mind are in a state of constant interaction. The process of *blending* the two using the art of meditation will ultimately make it difficult to differentiate them . . . in other words, you'll have reached a state of oneness. When you achieve this state, you'll be free to explore your soul further and attain a deeper understanding of your true self. The more you connect with your soul, the more likely you are to remember your Divine nature. You'll discover who you really are and realize that you're always connected to the universal energies that are present, both to help and guide you.

I want to encourage you once again to start meditating as much as possible in the same place and at the same time every day. By doing so, you'll increase the peaceful energy vibrations within and around your space. These frequencies will continue to build up over time so that when you walk in, you'll feel that positive energy, and entering a state of relaxation and meditation becomes a quicker and easier process.

EXERCISE: Relaxing the Body

This is a simple exercise to assist you in relaxing your body and preparing yourself for meditation. It's designed to help you increase your bodily awareness.

Before you start, get comfortable: Make sure that you're wearing loose-fitting clothing to prevent any physical restrictions. Sit comfortably in a straight-back chair, with your feet flat on the ground and your hands resting on your lap. For this exercise, it's better to sit rather than lie down, as I don't want you nodding off to sleep. It's important for you to be alert and aware when you're meditating. Good, now that we've established the ground rules, let's begin. . . .

Close your eyes and breathe in slowly, then exhale all that tension. Once again, breathe. Gently move all the parts of your body as you settle into a relaxed state. Try to become aware of your left foot, and slowly focus your attention there, tensing and relaxing that area. Gradually move your attention up your left leg and notice if there's any tightness in this region. If so, raise your leg and try tensing the muscles, then releasing them and relaxing.

Continue breathing as you slowly let your awareness travel up your left side, into your abdominal area, up to your chest, to your shoulder, and then down your left arm all the way to your fingers. Clench your left hand into a fist, and then relax it. Move your awareness up your arm again to your shoulder, down your neck, and all the way down your back. Wherever you're feeling strain, just tense the muscles, release them, and relax — then move on. Good, now slowly direct your awareness up to your head, scalp, and face and let go of any tightness in your jaw. Release any tension and feel the sense of relaxation take over.

Once you've worked up the left side, do the same thing for the right side, but this time start from the head, then move down your right shoulder, arm, hand, thigh, calf, foot, and on to your toes. Yet again, let your awareness slowly scan your whole body and see if there's a place that's calling out for attention. Always release the tension and relax.

Notice if there's still any tightness in a certain area, and if so, tense and gently release. Ask your body if that particular spot is holding on to a past memory or an emotion that needs to be released. There's no need to rush. Try to detect the specific part of your body that requires attention or effort to relax. Take your time and spend a moment with that area, letting the healing relaxation move through it and on to the rest of the body.

If you're feeling stressed or tense, this simple exercise will benefit you greatly in releasing the strain. At the same time, it will make it easier for you to practice future meditations.

EXERCISE: Stilling the Mind

As with all exercises, it's best to first get yourself situated in your personal space. Afterward, I want you to close your eyes and simply focus on your breath. Take your time. Each inhalation will bring more and more relaxation; and with each exhalation, I want you to let go of all stresses and tension.

Try this for five minutes, focusing on the regular rhythm of your breathing. You'll become increasingly relaxed with each breath. Just allow it to happen . . . let it all go and relax. If your mind starts to wander, just bring your focus back to your breath. If thoughts come in, acknowledge them and watch them leave again. Notice how it feels to be completely relaxed. Continue to focus on your breath while you let all the mind chatter slow down and evaporate.

Now, in your mind's eye, which is located in the area between your eyebrows (known as "the third eye"), I want you to imagine a symbol of your choosing. It can be a flower, a religious figure or icon, a single word, or whatever is pleasing to you. Make it your own special image that you'll use every time you meditate. At this point, just focus without straining on your chosen symbol. Good, now slowly inhale — but this time, bring your awareness up to your third eye as you concentrate on your symbol. It's almost as if you're breathing in and out through this center. Do this for another five minutes. If your mind wanders, return your focus to the breath, and allow your symbol to bring you back.

While you're in this relaxed state, it's a perfect time to ask your higher self for an answer to a specific question. You could get a message in any number of ways: You might see an image, a scene, or beautiful colors; or your spirit guides could make themselves known to you. The answer may not be immediate — sometimes it might come to you a few days later. Equally, you may be at the right place at the right time to receive your answer straightaway.

After about 15 minutes, wiggle your fingers as you shift your awareness to your body, and start to bring yourself back and become aware of the room around you. Remain seated for a moment, and allow your consciousness to fully absorb your meditation so that you remember how calm you felt having achieved the process of stilling the mind. In this peaceful state, anything is possible!

Meditation is an amazing practice because it's filled with many wonderful surprises. If you try it before you go to sleep at night, a dream may even provide you with answers. For this reason, it's helpful to keep your journal nearby after your meditation and beside the bed when you wake up in the morning. Remember that it's a good idea to write down everything in your journal when you first open your eyes in the morning — even prior to your feet touching the floor — before your mind brings you back into a state of full consciousness.

Soul Senses

We're born psychically aware, but all too quickly as we grow up, our minds are filled with external influences fed by teachers and parents, as well as the media. Our creative, intuitive right brain gets used less and less as the left side (the more analytical one) starts to take over. The result is that we pay less attention to our intuition to help guide us, and rely more and more on the outside world and our physical senses to make decisions — that is, we learn to rationalize.

Fortunately for us, from artists, teachers, builders, and administrative assistants to musicians and even authors, we're all unique and possess our own individual "special gifts" and talents. The same can be said for our psychic abilities. Each and every one of us will receive information in different ways, depending on our specific psychic strength.

After studying intuitive awareness for many years, I've learned that we all have one or more psychic abilities. In this chapter, I want to focus on the three most popular and widely used ones, which you'll be able to access once you've identified your individual psychic strength. These abilities are known as *clairsentience, clairvoyance,* and *clairaudience.*

It's quite natural that some of you will be more proficient in one area or another. If you think that your individual psychic aptitude is to become a *feeler,* then you should work to strengthen that ability before you start developing your other senses. I've noticed that many students who participate in my workshops believe that *seeing* is the best way to receive psychic information, but being a good *feeler* can also produce excellent results. With time and practice, along with some patience, it will be possible to use all three major psychic senses so that they work in unison. However, as you're starting out, I want you to discover and work with your primary *strength* at first. This is the best way to begin building a solid foundation with your own psychic self.

Now, let's explore and understand the workings of these abilities, and discover just how many you actually possess.

Clairsentience, or Clear Feeling

Clairsentience is the inner sense of *knowing*. It's one of the more familiar intuitive abilities and is relatively easy to develop and access. For example, have you ever walked into a room where an argument has recently taken place and you just feel it? Do you know why this is so? When the energy lingers, through your clairsentient ability, you end up sensing the emotions that led to the disagreement. In other words, you're *feeling* the turbulent, negative energy of that recent dispute.

Here's another example: Let's say that you're introduced to someone for the first time at a social gathering and you immediately get a feeling of discomfort or uneasiness. It's not so hard to grasp what you're sensing — you just *know* that you're not really going to bond with that person. It's a gut reaction, but you might tend to rationalize it by telling yourself that you probably just don't have anything in common with that individual. What's actually happening is that you're receiving thoughts and feelings from that person's aura, which are then transmitted through your solar plexus (one of the chakras), located in the abdominal area, resulting in what is so often called that "gut feeling," which in this case is a form of clairsentience.

Indicators of Being Clairsentient

- Are your feelings hurt easily?

- When meeting someone, do you intuitively know that something is wrong, even though the other person appears happy?

- When you're driving, do you instinctively sense when you should take a different route, only to find out later that you would have encountered a terrible traffic jam had you taken the original one?

- Are you the individual people go to when they're feeling down or need to get something off their chest?

- Do strangers often come up to you and ask for directions? Also, when shopping in a store, do people think that you're an employee and begin to ask you questions?

These are just a few of the possible signs of a clairsentient's sensitivity. People are naturally drawn to those with this ability. *Feelers* will also often receive other people's *stuff.* By "stuff," I mean information that's not yours. If your natural psychic inclination is to *feel,* it's also likely that you'll pick up vibrations from others, which will have an effect on your own disposition. There's a cautionary note that I need to include here. If your temperament is usually one that's upbeat, and for some inexplicable reason you start feeling down (even though nothing has happened around you to cause this), try approaching the phenomenon from a different angle: Instead of wondering, *What's wrong with me?* try asking yourself, *Who's wrong with me?*

It's often the case that you're actually tuning in to the feelings or vibrations from someone else without even knowing it. Your psychic ability can, and *wants,* to help that person. Next time this happens, just stop for a few minutes, focus on your solar-plexus area, and pose the question: *Whose feelings are these?* As you do, see if someone's image comes to mind. It could be anyone, from a member of your family to a best friend, a neighbor, or even a co-worker. Try calling whoever it is, and casually ask how he or she is doing. You may be surprised to find out that the other person is the one who's feeling down. If you're clairsentient, it's likely that you'll pick up other people's emotions whether they're happy *or* sad.

We live in a society where people are less prone to hugging, touching, and embracing each other. If you're clairsentient, you *need* to feel things physically. This benefits your intuitive psychic ability and helps you understand someone on a much deeper soul level — in other words, you make a *soul-to-soul* connection. The hands are wonderful receptors of energy. The next time you meet someone new, look into this person's eyes, reach out, shake hands, and form a *real* bond. Equally, when you encounter friends, give them a big hug. Just being aware of your clairsentience and the subtle ways in which you receive information will help you so much, providing a wonderful tool to assist you in finding the answers to those unresolved questions.

EXERCISE: Opening the Soul Sense of *Inner Feeling*

When you're about to make an important decision, whether it's about a new relationship, buying a car or a home, changing jobs, or a business matter, focus on your clairsentient conduit — your solar plexus — and try the following exercise (once you're settled in your personal space).

Close your eyes and hold your hands over your solar-plexus area. Imagine that this part of your body is slowly filling up with beautiful yellow light. When you feel relaxed and comfortable, ask yourself: *How do I feel about this decision?* or *How do I feel about this person?* See if an emotion or an image comes to mind. Ask yourself, *Does this feel positive or negative?* If you're uncomfortable with what you're feeling, then inquire: *Why am I uneasy?* The more specific the question, the more specific the answer. This exercise only takes a few minutes!

Here's another great exercise that's saved me from spending a lot of time reproaching myself unnecessarily for other people's actions. When you sense or feel a negative mood emanating from someone, try this useful technique to understand what's going on with this person, before you blame yourself. First, get *yourself* out of your own way. Discard the thoughts relating to what you're perceiving or feeling. Relax, close your eyes, and breathe. Try to imagine that you're literally stepping into the other individual's shoes and becoming that person. Feel what he or she is feeling. See if you now have a better understanding of what's *really* happening and how you could possibly help.

Now that you have a rudimentary grasp of clairsentience and know how to access it, experiment in any area of your life that you wish. This ability can become highly tuned — or if necessary, you can turn it down to decrease your psychic sensitivity . . . just focus on your solar plexus, and imagine the yellow light getting smaller. Once you've practiced working with your clairsentience, try going for walks in the country, opening yourself up to experiencing the outdoors and all its beauty. Since everything is made up of energy, you'll quickly learn to feel it all.

Clairvoyance, or Clear Seeing

Clairvoyance is the inner sense of *seeing*. It's when you receive information in the form of images, symbols, and colors. It's not about seeing in the physical sense with your eyes; it's about using your *inner* sight, better known as "the third eye." The soul never speaks without a picture.

Many psychics and mediums see subjectively (in their own mind) in this way. Sometimes you may notice them looking away when they're giving a reading. When I create a psychic link with spirit on the Other Side, I'm known to glance over my left shoulder. It's not that I don't want to make eye contact with the sitter (the person I'm reading for) — rather, it's that I'm looking at a blank screen with my third eye. I refer to this as my "psychic screen," and for me, it's almost as though a mini-movie is playing out right in front of me. Over the years, I've honed this skill and developed the ability to see the images with greater clarity and definition.

Sometimes in the early stages of development, the images can be fleeting or quite subtle. That's why most people don't even notice them, and they're easily missed. A popular misconception I've heard is that a 3-D rift is going to open up right in front of them when a clairvoyant vision comes. In reality, it's more about receiving symbols, images, and sometimes words. As I've said, each of us has a unique interpretation of these symbols. Through time and practice, the same ones will repeatedly come back to you clairvoyantly, and you'll learn how to make sense of them by drawing your own analogies and personal reference points. It's important to make a note of these patterns in your journal and see if they feel right to you. As they build up, they'll become your own *psychic dictionary* for interpreting clairvoyant information.

Indicators of Being Clairvoyant

• Do you often experience vivid, highly memorable dreams?

• Are you the sort of person who doesn't wear a watch, because you have the ability to picture the correct time?

• Are you good at visualizing exactly where to place furniture to enhance the energy flow or the aesthetics of a room?

• Can you look at people and know that they're coming down with something even though they appear quite healthy?

• When talking on the phone, are you able to envision what the other person looks like, even though you've never met before?

If you've answered yes to some or all of these questions, then you could already possess some clairvoyant ability. Don't let any popular misconceptions hinder your personal development. Some people can find the unknown a little scary — the word *clairvoyant* itself might act as deterrent. It's easy to be influenced by TV shows, which portray clairvoyants with cliché-ridden images of smoke-filled rooms and crystal balls. I think it's time to dispel those myths.

Clairvoyance is merely seeing through your mind's eye. To be a little more scientific, the reception area for this ability is situated between your brows (the third-eye chakra), and is associated with the pituitary gland. People who display a strong tendency toward being clairvoyant often want to spend time in big, open, well-lit spaces. Likewise, when they travel, they're the ones who have to see it all, as though they can't bear to miss anything! As with clairsentience, using your clairvoyant ability can benefit you as well as others, once you know how to access the specific reception area and interpret your own symbols and images.

I heard a wonderful story recently from man named Jack. While sitting in his living room, Jack looked up at a newly bought picture of an angel that his wife had proudly hung right over their fireplace. While staring at this piece of art and trying to figure out if he liked it or not, he noticed that the face of the angel began to blur and change. He somehow recognized a new face take form right in front of him. He blinked a few times to see if that would clear his vision, but the image before him continued to change. He noticed that the angel was starting to resemble his Aunt Mary, whom he hadn't seen in a while. He told himself that he was seeing things and it was all his imagination, chalking it up to the fact that he'd had a long day. After all, he wasn't into all that stuff, as he jokingly explained to me.

The next day he was perplexed, as he couldn't get the image of his aunt's face out of his mind. He called up his cousin Carol, who was Mary's daughter. He knew that Carol was more knowledgeable about such metaphysical incidents. He proceeded to warily tell his story to her. Now, Carol knew for a fact that Jack wasn't into making up stories, so she called her mother to see how she was doing. Mary said that she was fine but explained that she'd been feeling a little dizzy lately. Carol decided to take her in for a checkup the next day, just as a precaution.

Well, I think that you know where this story is going. The doctor ran all his tests, and Mary was diagnosed with abnormally high blood pressure and was immediately given medication to lower it. It was Jack's clairvoyant image and the actions that followed that got his aunt medical care before her health condition caused a potentially serious situation.

A great way to train and sharpen your clairvoyance is to listen to meditation tapes using visualization techniques that take you on a beautiful journey in your mind's eye. As part of my teachings, I recommend that whenever you spend time outside, you might try to pay attention to everything around you, whether it's the deep blue of the sky or the calming green of the grass and trees. Try to notice all the diverse cultures and people you're exposed to each and every day. When they're developing this ability, so many people want to see with their psychic eye immediately, whereas I

believe that it's important to start by looking around and noticing one's surroundings right here in the physical world. If you
follow my advice, you'll be training your eyes and your mind to
observe more, which will assist you in developing your clairvoyant
strength.

Try the following exercise to understand where your psychic
eye is located, as this technique will help you expand your inner
vision.

EXERCISE: Opening the Soul Sense of *Inner Vision*

As before, get yourself situated. For this exercise, you'll need a
small white votive candle. Sit comfortably with the burning candle
in front of you. Relax your eyes and stare into the flame. You'll
feel your eyes start to water; when they do, close them and put the
palms of your hands over your eyes to create a total blackout. You
should now start to notice that the flame is flickering slightly above
and between your brows. Wait until it disappears, then repeat the
exercise for another 10 to 15 minutes. What you're actually doing is
training and developing your clairvoyant eye. Now you know that
this special spot is just above the bridge of your nose, *not* where
you look straight out with your physical vision.

The next time you want to use your psychic abilities to help
answer a question or make a decision, start by closing your eyes
and gently focusing on your third-eye area. Then go ahead and
ask what you need to. (Remember to be as specific as possible.)
Write down the original question in your journal along with the
response, whether you saw a symbol, a word, a color, a person, or
even an object. By practicing and experimenting, you'll continue
to sharpen this ability.

Start off small with some simple tests — for example, try to
guess the suit of playing cards after turning them upside down.
I used to play the following game with my mother when I was a
child (little did I know I was training my psychic abilities at that
young age!). Have a friend think of a number from 1 to 50, and
see if you can visualize it. Go with the first answer that pops into

your psychic vision. Another great experiment is to have someone stand in another room and choose something to hold in his or her hands. From the room where you are, make a mental note of what you see, whether it's an image or an outline. Trust what you're receiving before your logical mind tries to shoot it down.

These exercises may seem elementary, but what's actually happening is that you're beginning to stretch your abilities once again. Now you'll appreciate the saying "Use it or lose it"! You can make up your own experiments, since there's so much more to see once you learn to harness this remarkable ability.

Clairaudience, or Clear Hearing

Clairaudience is the inner sense of *hearing*. It's the ability to hear names; dates; certain sayings; and yes, even songs and melodies. When you hear *subjectively* (in other words, in your mind), you're aware of sounds as though they were words spoken in your own voice. This is why it can be a little confusing to determine if these are your own thoughts or psychic ones. However, with practice, you'll be able to differentiate between the two. It's also important to point out that some people hear *objectively* — that is, outside of themselves.

Have you ever heard your name called out, only to find out that no one was there? It may be from a loved one in spirit, or it might be somebody here on Earth who's thinking of you. If you feel that it's the latter, try calling whoever it is to say hi. Most likely, the person will tell you that he or she was just thinking of you.

Another good example of clairaudience is when you hear a song playing in your head. Stop for a minute, and make a mental note of what tune it is. Listen to the words, because all too often there could be a message of encouragement or advice for you or someone close to you who needs a lift or a helping hand. When I do readings for people on the telephone, I'll use my clairaudient ability by tuning in to the energy via their voice, which is a powerful medium for picking up intuitive information. The next time you're on the phone with someone, close your eyes and really listen to the voice on the other end. Let the person's tone and words completely enter your space so that your intuition takes over for your conscious reaction. You may notice colors, images, or even feelings that have nothing to do with the conversation. So don't just listen with your ears . . . listen with your intuition.

This ability can be accessed through the throat reception area (throat chakra), and clairaudients can increase their psychic *listening strength* by focusing on this region of the body.

Indicators of Being Clairaudient

- Do you always think inside your head instead of out loud?

- Can you tell when someone isn't telling the truth?

- Are you attracted to loud places?

- Do you have music playing in the background no matter what you're doing?

- Do you ever hear what others are thinking?

Clairaudience is that small voice that you so often hear — the one that so many of us don't listen to enough, only to regret it later.

The first stage of developing your clairaudient ability is learning to differentiate psychic information from your everyday thoughts and mind chatter. To do so, you'll need to practice steadily improving your clairaudience. Over time, the information you receive via your *inner voice* will start to flow and develop a sharper sense of clarity. Generally, this input should always be for the highest good and have a *positive* tone to it. If you're receiving *negative* information, then most likely there's some interference from your own mind. In this instance, you should consider checking to see if there are emotional or psychological issues that need addressing before you continue.

One very important piece of advice that I give people who are beginning their psychic training is this: When you believe that you're receiving psychic data, step back and ask yourself, *Is this information coming to me or from me?* In doing so, you'll help keep a firm balance with your psychic development and remain subjective at all times.

As you develop further, you'll be able to access your psychic hearing to assist you in many areas of your life. If clairaudience is *your strength,* then try the following exercises.

EXERCISE 1: Opening the Soul Sense of *Inner Hearing*

This time, I want you to find a comfortable place outdoors such as a park or the beach — somewhere that people of all ages come together. Sit down on a nice bench, under a tree, or in another location that feels comfortable. Good, now close your eyes, breathe in slowly, and relax. That's it . . . just relax. Now, I don't want you to *look,* but rather, to *listen* with your physical hearing. Try to focus on the sounds from far off. See if you can hear the traffic, a plane, or voices of people talking. Reach out as far as you can with your hearing. Good. Now slowly bring your awareness closer to your surroundings. Can you hear children playing? Are other people speaking? Try to figure out the age difference in their voices — are they young or old? Are there birds in the area? Notice all sounds, far and near, at the same time. Now, while this is happening, try to listen to the silence in between the sounds. This is the special place where the undercurrent of intuitive information can often be picked up.

What you're doing with this exercise is training your physical hearing to reach different levels and ranges. I may use the word *hearing,* but it's really more about *listening* to receive impressions. There's a big difference between hearing and listening, so try to understand the distinction. In doing so, you'll actually sharpen your soul sense of clairaudience and become more familiar with that still, small voice within. Listen carefully, for often the soul speaks to you in a whisper.

EXERCISE 2: Inner Hearing

Sit or lie down in a comfortable, quiet position. Take a deep breath, letting the day slip away. Close your eyes and relax. Now, slowly imagine a beautiful sky-blue light situated in your throat area. Imagine that this illumination is slowly expanding as you breathe into this center. This is the place where clairaudience is accessed.

Take a few moments here to ask any question that you'd like information or guidance on, but as you're doing so, keep your awareness concentrated in this area and on the sky-blue light. Don't be put off if at first you don't hear anything. You may eventually receive a word or even a sentence. Does the answer you obtain relate to the question you asked? If you don't understand it, ask yourself: *What does this mean to me?* More information could flow, or your inner guidance might want to stick to the answer it originally gave. Trust what you're receiving, for you may notice at a later date or time that it was the perfect response.

Next time you're about to go into a meeting, take a few moments to focus on your throat area, and ask: *What do I need to know for this meeting?* A word of advice, a song, or even a symbol that somehow seems to speak to you in its own way may emerge. Your angels and guides are also waiting to assist you — all you have to do is ask and listen for their messages. In your journal, make a note of what you're receiving and date it, because you may receive information that doesn't make sense at the time but falls into place later. As I've said before, don't forget to ask, *Is this coming <u>to</u> me or <u>from</u> me?*

I wrote earlier that being psychic is a way of being. Making time for activities that contribute to your spiritual growth and intuitive development isn't a sign of selfishness, but it will have a major impact on your overall well-being and spiritual vitality. Spending a few moments focusing on your soul's needs enables you to nurture yourself and expand your spiritual boundaries. Therefore, for just one week, I want you to do things that are uncharacteristic of you — in other words, activities that you don't normally do. During this test week, you're going to trust your intuitive psychic abilities completely.

For example, if you've always wanted to have lunch with someone at work but never made the effort, then let this be the week to ask. If you feel drawn to call a relative you haven't spoken to in a long time, pick up the phone. If there's a road that you always wanted to drive down on your way home from work but never did, take that route now. Is there a book that you always wanted to read but never went out to get? . . . Well, you know what I'm trying to say.

I want you to trust and follow your gut using all your soul senses. After practicing this for one week, write in your journal about any new discoveries or revelations that resulted from following your inner guidance. Sometimes when you listen to the prompting of your soul, it could easily lead to other opportunities. This amazing exercise will teach you how the flow of intuition runs through you and works *for* you. What I'm actually trying to do here is to get you to live intuitively and less analytically . . . go for it!

As you learn to reawaken and develop your individual psychic ability — whether it's clairsentience, clairvoyance, or clairaudience — please remember to stay grounded and balanced. When this inner guidance is properly honed, it can greatly assist you in all areas of your life, but most important, it will benefit your spiritual development. It should be a wonderful experience and a journey as you discover and build up your soul senses. Flex those intuitive muscles! The more you use them, the stronger they'll get.

Chakras: The Spiritual Batteries of the Soul

Humans continually seek out different places to find enlightenment, whether it's a church, a synagogue, or one of the many sacred locations all over the world. We persistently search for our own soul or some type of spiritual source, and as a result, we have a tendency to look outside ourselves. I certainly don't undervalue the importance many people put on these places of worship, as I often visit churches myself for wisdom, peace, and solitude — an activity I find comforting and uplifting. However, when you begin to understand and work with the chakra system, you'll soon realize and appreciate that the body is truly *your* temple.

I remember the first time that I heard the word *chakra* — it was one of those words that was immediately lodged in my consciousness. I was intrigued by every aspect of it, from the sound itself to its origin and meaning. I made a promise to myself that I'd discover and learn exactly what this intriguing term truly meant. Of course, I didn't realize at the time what an important and fascinating function the chakras serve for our overall well-being. (As I mentioned, a more in-depth look at them can be found in my second book, *Psychic Navigator.*)

The chakras are the energy centers of the body, but I often refer to them as our "spiritual batteries." *Chakra* is a Sanskrit word meaning "wheel." Some people prefer to imagine chakras as beautiful lotuses with unfolding petals, while others who've developed their psychic sight may see them as vortices of swirling light.

Evidence of these energy centers has been documented for thousands of years in the East, and only more recently in the West. We're now investigating and researching this precious energy system and discovering that the body *is* a vehicle of consciousness. Everyone I've ever met or studied with over the years as I've developed my psychic and mediumistic abilities has come to the same conclusion, one that I firmly hold to be true: Our anatomy is engineered by a complex network of etheric wiring to aid the flow of energy, and the chakras are the organizing centers for both the reception and the transmission of life energies (chi/prana) — which are essential to the development of our body, mind, soul, and spirit.

There are *seven* major chakras (as well as many minor ones) within and around you. Each corresponds to an endocrine gland in your body. During the early stages of your development, I suggest that you focus on these seven main centers.

The chakras run upward along the spinal cord. Energy enters

from both the front and back of each one. Chakras are the link between your *physical body* and your *aura,* and they constantly interact with one another. Each one is complemented by a distinctive auric color and has its own unique function. The seven centers act as sensitive contact points, or bridges where the physical and the spiritual worlds meet. The lower chakras deal with the body and relate to issues of living in the material world, such as survival, health, careers, safety, and the home. The upper or higher chakras deal with all psychic abilities and spiritual gifts.

Your actions and thoughts play a big part in controlling this flow of energy, as well as the functions of the chakras. Even though the energy that runs through these centers remains constant, it can be increased or decreased, depending on how well you balance your life. For instance, if you're worrying about money matters (earthly, *physical* concerns), then your *lower* chakras are likely to be affected in a negative way, slowing down their *rate* and *spin.* When this happens, the dispersal of energy will be weaker, and as a result, you may feel sluggish or out of balance.

In contrast, when you're feeling compassionate toward someone — or if you're focusing on higher spiritual thoughts — then the *upper* chakras are more apt to spin freely, resulting in the energy being distributed easily, with a sense of harmony and vitality. There has to be *balance* when you activate and work with your chakras. You should never focus on stimulating just one; all seven of them should be in balance so that the flow of energy can travel through them evenly to the appropriate areas.

I believe that you're meant to have unlimited amounts of energy and should be able to tap into your creative talents easily, as well as live a life of love, compassion, and most important . . . peace. It's possible to gain powerful guidance for your life once you turn inward and consult your inner wisdom. By allowing the natural balance of energies to flow through your spiritual batteries — where transformation truly begins — you'll be able to hear, see, and feel the voice of your higher self with greater clarity. You'll intuitively have the power to make better choices and create a more fulfilling life.

⋮ ⋮ ⋮

CHAPTER FOUR

The Power of Love

To feel the power of love in our lifetime can be one of the most beautiful, significant, and life-changing events that we experience as a soul . . . yet it's so much more than just being able to say that we've cared for another person. Love isn't meant to be a destination; rather, it's about the journey. It's the path that we all hope to travel in this lifetime, the process of becoming the person we were meant to be — a person living and feeling from the heart and soul. When the energy of love is in our presence, we can all sense it moving within us. Somehow, this emotion has a way of showing us that we're connected to something much larger than ourselves.

We've developed technologies to send people to the moon, wipe out certain diseases through medical and scientific achievements, and erect huge monuments and buildings. In addition, we now use the Internet to communicate with friends and family on the other side of the globe in a matter of seconds. We constantly embrace new advancements. We can be a wonderful race, with the capacity to do so much, yet some of us are incapable of the one thing that should come quite naturally to us — giving and receiving love. This inability can result from the fact we weren't loved in the past or have been hurt and let down. It can also be caused by loneliness, insecurity, or the fear of being vulnerable.

Love is the foundation of your existence, and you're just as capable of giving it as you are of receiving it. Love can be a beautiful emotion, but it's also a form of energy that propels you through life. It's truly the power of the soul, for when it's received, it radiates through your heart center in a constant state of motion. Everything in your energetic system revolves around the heart center. You can liken this part of you to your own personal sun: Is it any wonder that when you see certain metaphysical drawings, they portray rays of light emanating from the center of the figure's chest? It's the location of your being — your very core — and is the place where your soul's wisdom resides. I once read: "To be a master of the heart, one must live from the heart."

This special center represents unconditional love, compassion, joy, balance, relationships, and healing. It's the link running from your mind, body, and soul to spirit. Of course, this center is associated with the human heart, so it's quite likely that you've heard some of the popular expressions that convey this sentiment, such as "That person has such an open heart!" "Why is he closing off his heart to me?" "I'm suffering from a broken heart," or the ever-popular "I love you with all my heart."

The heart center can be filled with so much joy and happiness, since your feelings flow through it. It's also a repository for all past hurts, disappointments, and emotional scars. Have you ever meditated and started to get emotional or even begun to cry? The reason is that spiritual energy is reaching out and touching your heart center — it's trying to move it, to help clear the blockages that have been stuck or held there so that healing can begin. These blockages could have originated as recently as last week, or they may be from years and years ago.

Love reveals itself in many forms, and we experience it on many levels. Generally, if we're loved, then we feel safe. Likewise, if we're in a loving environment, we feel nurtured. We tend to cherish our animals, our creative work, the earth, and being out in nature — or, in fact, anything that makes our heart and soul sing. Love can soothe, comfort, uplift, and heal us.

Your soul cares for you and wants nothing in return — its love is unconditional. No matter what you've done or others have done to you, it's the heart center that's affected. In order to give and receive love, you have to open this part of you. You're a being of light, energy, and compassion; therefore, these are the forces that you must bring into your heart center. When it's open and the blockages have been cleared, healing can begin in all areas of your life. When this happens, you'll be in a better place to happily and healthfully lend your gifts and talents to others. As you heal, you'll create and accomplish your life purpose of being all that you can be, offering a valued service to humanity. This is the totality of your creative existence.

The following meditation will assist you in opening your heart center. It's important to go at your own pace and do the exercise as many times as you feel comfortable. Feelings will surface as the spiritual energy flows through you, moving and clearing blockages that may be holding you back. When you open yourself up to the power of love, you can cherish yourself and others, along with the world and everything in it. Love has the power to show you that you're so much more than your conscious mind perceives you to be.

Let's begin the journey of letting the energy of *love* enter your heart and your life, allowing you to receive and give this emotion and to radiate as the pure soul that you truly are.

Loving-Kindness Meditation

When you connect, listen to, and follow your heart and soul, you're linking and blending with the Divine Source, and you're reminded of your own true perfection and Divinity. This heart-center exercise is a technique that's based on a Buddhist meditation to release sadness and fear and bring compassion and love into your life. Not only does it benefit you, but it also assists the people around you. It can be used to bring peace and harmony to a situation and help instill positive thinking and upliftment into the heart and soul.

Sit in a comfortable position with your back straight, but don't lie down. Relax your head and shoulders. Now, close your eyes and breathe slowly . . . just breathe. Allow your body to simply relax. If you feel any stress or tightness, imagine it being released as you exhale. Take your time as you relax and breathe away the different tension spots as you become aware of them, one by one. That's right — nice, slow breaths.

Now, place your left palm on the center of your chest, and then position your right palm over your left hand. Inhale deeply into your stomach, and let your breath ever so slowly rise up into your chest. Continue this form of breathing for a minute or two. As you simply focus on the breath, allow all your thoughts to go quiet and still. If thoughts bubble to the surface, just acknowledge them and let them go; don't pay any attention to them. Lightly focus on your breath as you inhale and exhale.

Next, with your eyes still closed, gently take your hands away from your chest and rub your palms together. This will make them warm as you infuse them with energy. Now, place your hands in the same position in the center of your chest again. Imagine this energy to be a bright emerald green light as it enters and fills your heart center and your whole chest area. Stay with this for a moment. When you're ready, let this emerald green energy fill your entire body. Feel it run up and down your spine nice and slowly. Take your time and breathe. Remain with this visualization for a few minutes.

Now, as you breathe out, imagine that the beautiful emerald green energy is assisting you in releasing negative emotions of anger, feelings of failure, and even criticisms of yourself and others. As you breathe in again, imagine the positive energies of the Divine Source — such as kindness, compassion, forgiveness, and love — flowing into your heart center. Let this energy permeate throughout your body, spreading into every muscle, fiber, nerve, and cell.

Focus your attention once again on your heart center. Breathe into this region. As you do so, you're in fact breathing energy and light into your soul. Experience and feel the positive energies flowing into this area. As you exhale, I now want you to concentrate and direct these positive energies into feelings of loving kindness and compassion that are pouring out from your heart center.

Send the energy out gradually rather than opening the floodgates all at once. First, place positive thoughts of love and kindness on yourself for a moment. Next, direct these thoughts to someone else whom you care about. Let your soul and heart energy blend with the other person's. Then aim the same thoughts of kindness at someone you feel neutral about — an individual you don't know very well. Use the first person who comes to mind. Once again, let your soul and heart energy blend with the other person's. Now, send these positive thoughts of love and kindness to someone you really dislike or have negative feelings toward. Merge the light from your heart and soul with that of the other person. Envision these thoughts as energy going out, and remain with each person for a moment or two.

As you finish, see these loving thoughts of kindness extending to a wider circle of your family, friends, and co-workers; people in your town, city, or village; and then your entire country — and finally, the whole world. You're light and love. Your heart and soul know no boundaries as they reach out, filling the planet with positive loving energy.

To close, bring your awareness back to yourself and to your heart center. Open your eyes, flex your fingers and toes, and ground yourself before you stand. This energy can result in a powerful meditation. The more you practice it and open yourself up to the different stages, the stronger the feelings of love and kindness will be.

Relationships of the Soul

I couldn't write a chapter on the energy of love without touching on relationships and how they unfold on a soul level. Relationships are mirror images for your own life — the way you feel and treat yourself, as well as how you react and respond to different situations and people around you. All relationships (whether they're on an emotional, physical, mental, or spiritual level) are part of the learning process and enlightenment of the soul. No matter which category one falls into, it acts as a teaching tool for you understand the lessons that your soul needs to master. It can help you understand, change, or enhance your individual qualities.

Every relationship is an opportunity for soul growth. Different types of relationships have an uncanny way of showing you what you need to work on in your life. At times, they reveal your vulner-abilities and insecurities or your need for attention, approval, and acceptance. Equally, they can identify where you may be stuck in a rut or where you lack love, peace, healing, or joy in your life.

Working as a psychic medium, I've come to appreciate and look at people on a soul level. This helps me express love through my heart and experience the interaction as a soul. When I'm faced with difficult people, I always attempt to connect with them on a soul level . . . in other words, I try to make a soul-to-soul connection. Trust me, I know that sometimes it's not that easy, but I look at them from a Divine perspective. I try to understand them through my own soul — my heart center — by tapping into and using my intuition. I view them as a Divine soul instead of what my eyes see or the reaction that's my conscious response. This enables me to see the *real* person and the good that I know is inside all of us. Occasionally, that Divinity — that goodness that I know is there — may be buried. Often it's suffocated by years of torment, negative behavior, mental conditioning, or unhealthy relationships.

Sometimes the most challenging and painful relationships can act as our best teachers and guides. Relationships of all kinds are really about *you,* even in the most difficult situations. As I've said, they're meant to be mirrors for us, always reflecting back what we need to see. The question is: "Do you want to look in this mirror and be open to what you need to learn, or simply pretend that it's not there and pass it by?"

Business relationships can certainly test you. A few years ago, I moved back to Massachusetts after living in California for many years. I took a job as an office manager for a high-powered busi-nessman who worked in the travel industry. It didn't take me long to settle into the new position, and I developed a good relation-ship with my boss. Everything seemed to start off really well, and I enjoyed the new job. However, after a few months, the relationship began to change as the respect he'd shown in those early months suddenly evaporated and was replaced by demands that were often barked across the room. My boss became more aggressive, and there were occasions when his temper got so bad that I didn't know what to do or expect. These were the times when I kept my head down!

I'm sure that this is an all-too-familiar story, but since I needed the job, I stayed on, suffering in silence.

Early one morning, I'd just returned to the office with my boss's morning coffee. He yelled another command from his office about his upcoming travel plans, departing in his usual whirlwind, without even a thank-you. As I sat there trembling and feeling upset, confused, and angry, I thought: *Why am I enduring this work relationship?* As soon as I asked the question, I *knew* the answer: I was reliving my whole childhood relationship with my father. I was so keen for approval and attention that I was allowing myself to be treated like a child all over again. It was totally unintentional, but at least I realized it before it was too late.

In my eyes, my boss and his behavior were a reflection of those challenging times I experienced as I was growing up: the alcoholic outbursts from my father after long drinking bouts, abuse in the form of a torrent of taunts and obscenities, being made to feel small, and living with the anxiety of never knowing what he was going to do next. I was reliving it all over again 20 years later. (Okay, there wasn't any alcohol involved, but the same feelings prevailed.) I'd inadvertently taken on the role of a child again. I thought that I'd worked through the issues of my relationship with my father, but apparently not — they'd risen to the surface again. The situation at work was sending an obvious signal to me about the relationship between my boss and me, and it was teaching me a painful lesson, yet one that I clearly needed to experience one more time. I realized that I still had to work on myself, my self-esteem, and my courage, as well as focus on the healing of my soul.

Unbelievably, as strange as it may sound, I actually thanked the Universe for what it was showing me. I forgave and extended gratitude to my boss within myself, and shortly afterward, I quit the job. The combination of moving on from that position and some intense work on myself enabled me to break the pattern that makes many of us fall into unhealthy relationships. I finally *got* the lesson.

Interestingly enough, that was the last job I had before I became a professional psychic medium. So, you can see why I thanked the Universe for the wonderful opportunity to advance myself.

Sometimes life has a way of putting the same lesson in front of you until you get it! If necessary, you'll find yourself in a recurring cycle until you finally learn how to deal with your issues. Really it's a way of life kicking you in the ass and helping you move to the next level! Today, my former employer and I get along great, and he's respectful of the work that I'm now doing.

If you look back on all your relationships, whatever the individual situations, you'll begin to see a pattern. The learning process is all part of guiding you in the direction of where you're supposed to be. If enough people constantly encourage you to change something in your life, take up a new hobby, or modify the way you approach life, perhaps there's a message there. Equally, a certain relationship can be the catalyst for a major shift.

I was 17 years old when a friend took me to see my first psychic. During the reading, I was told that I would live in California, I'd write books, and I was psychically gifted. Well, being a typical teenager, I just said, "Yeah, okay — *right.*"

That one incident was to be the start of a lifelong journey of learning and understanding as I became aware of spirituality and my own psychic gift. I often wonder what direction my life would have taken if my friend hadn't brought me to that psychic. Maybe I would have discovered my abilities and spirituality anyway, but much later in life. My friend will never know just how much of a catalyst she was for my development. Perhaps our relationship had been of two kindred souls connecting, and fate had played its part. When people hear the words *kindred souls,* they automatically think of a love connection. However, a kindred soul can also be someone who tests your very nerves but in the end stretches your potential beyond what you thought possible.

Everyone has had these types of relationships — you just need to take the time to look into your past. Please remember that not *all* relationships have to be one-on-one with just a single individual. They can be with a group, an organization, a pet, or even an incident or situation. Write down in your journal the relationships you've had in the past, and see if they've guided you in the direction of where you are now — or did they lead you away from your purpose? On another page, write down all the relationships that are happening in your life right now. Ask yourself the following questions:

- What am I learning from this relationship?

- What qualities am I developing?

- Is this relationship for my highest good?

- How can I make this relationship better?

- Is there an even exchange of energy?

- Are we learning from each other?

- What have I discovered, or am still discovering, about myself through this relationship?

- Are the people in my life empowering and encouraging me to be all that I can be?

Within every relationship, there's an encoded lesson that you've hopefully learned, or still need to learn. Some relationships are simply there for you to experience love; others could be showing you what you *don't* want in your next one. In this way, when it's time to develop a connection with someone else, you'll be more aware and have the ability to manifest the type of relationship you want — one that serves your highest purpose. Whatever the case, when you learn to open your heart and view it through the eyes of your soul, you'll discover an even better relationship that's waiting for you: the relationship of your soul-self.

Soul Solitude

Phones ringing, e-mails to be sent, pagers going off, bumper-to-bumper traffic, televisions blaring — stress and noise everywhere!

This is how most of us now lead our lives. With this constant racket, the continual distractions, our busy schedules, and the hustle and bustle of everyday life, how can we even begin to be with ourselves? How can we connect with our soul or block out the background noise long enough to hear the inside wisdom that our soul is trying to pass on? When we become more aware of our soul and heart, we strengthen the link with the Divine Source, and we're reminded once again of our true perfection.

On a physical level, it's easy to get caught up in the material world, but occasionally it's important to step back from your outside world to give yourself a chance to pause, reflect, and heal. You need to schedule some alone time so that you can commune with your soul and give the power of spirit the time and opportunity to restore energy and vitality to you. Sometimes when work obligations have been intense, you can feel so stressed and worn-out that you just need to get away from it all. I'm not talking about a typical vacation, but rather, something on a more spiritual level, such as a retreat — a place to rejuvenate your energy, release those tensions, and quiet your mind.

Vacations generally cater to our physical pleasure senses, instead of feeding the inner-self. We go on them for the purposes of sightseeing, dancing, drinking, sunbathing, shopping, and packing as much as we can into such a short time. How many times have you gone on a trip and said: "I need a vacation from my vacation!"?

Retreats and vacations have such different purposes and outcomes. All some people want to do is rest. That's fine, but when I refer to a *retreat*, I think of a place where you can spend time, stepping back from the pressures and distractions of everyday life. Retreats enable you to be quiet, unplug, relish the solitude, journal your thoughts, and most important, be in communion with yourself. By devoting time to strengthening the connection between your body, mind, and spirit, you create a harmonious balance that permeates all areas of your life. This time offers you a chance to look inward to connect with your spiritual center for self-discovery and clarification. When it's time to go back to your routine, you'll have a clearer perspective on *how* you live, as well as a more positive focus on the direction for the future. This confident attitude will spread to other areas of your life, and hopefully you'll continue this ritual of self-improvement and better self-care.

Retreats aren't necessarily about the *quantity* of time; it's more the *quality* of time that you spend on yourself that counts. I often teach at the Omega Institute in upstate New York, which offers workshops, retreats, and wellness vacations. It's set among beautiful gardens and rolling hills, next to a spectacular lake. The institute's mission "to create a peaceful oasis in a hurried world" is certainly fulfilled in this respect.

I was teaching a course on psychic development, and during one of the breaks, I took a walk on the grounds for a little fresh air before the next segment of my class. It was a beautiful summer day, and there were lots of people of all ages taking a break: Some were sitting against a tree, writing in their journals; some were meditating; and others were lying on their backs, staring up at the sky. I also noticed that a few people were quietly walking around with their heads bowed. There's nothing unusual about this, except that in this case, these people weren't in my class. I found out later that these students were participating in another workshop, and they were practicing their silent period. They were instructed not to talk, engage, or interact with anyone else for about three hours. . . . If you think that this is easy, then try it and see for yourself!

Most of us are constantly interacting with others all day, but when we're not doing so, we're inside our own heads, talking to ourselves and always thinking, thinking, thinking. The purpose of not speaking to anyone, which is a form of solitude, is to let our minds bring up thoughts without paying attention to them as we let them come and go.

If you practice these quiet times, you'll find that the hold that your mind has over you will diminish. The constant mind chatter will ebb like an outgoing tide. In other words, you begin to have control over your thoughts, instead of them controlling you. This is when you start to hear your own inner voice and value the stillness that results from solitude.

As the weekend drew to a close, I noticed how all the people on the campus appeared really peaceful and serene, with a twinkle in their eyes as though there was a light illuminating them. I believe that this is when your soul is beaming and saying, "I'm happy!"

By going on a retreat and spending time in quiet contemplation, we're giving ourselves a chance to be with our soul, in nature and in the now. It's a great way of releasing those stored-up tensions and irritations that we may have been holding on to. More and more of us are seeking answers and looking for the tools to find our own inner-self, but with our busy lifestyles and schedules, rarely do we take the time to notice the outer beauty that surrounds us.

When you stop for a moment without all the distractions, you'll have time to reflect on the individuals and situations in your life and how you *feel* about them. This can be quite cathartic, as you filter out what's working from what's not. It's a way of dealing with, releasing, and purging the things that have been consuming your vital soul energy and holding you back from living the life you want. Just as you clear your physical spaces of clutter, the energetic fields that are a vital part of your well-being must be cleansed of disruptive energies and emotions. This is a way of restoring the connection with yourself and your Divine inner wisdom.

Retreats don't have to be luxurious spas or hidden away in the hills. They can be simple places yet still be a vacation for the soul. When a friend of mine named David takes a retreat to be with himself and his soul in solitude, he goes to a local monastery run by Franciscan monks. Many such monasteries allow people to come and spend time in quiet contemplation. The lifestyle there is exactly what David needs. The monks let him spend time alone in meditation, prayer, and silence — they're not there to convert him, but rather, to honor his request as a spiritual being.

Solitude is recognized, revered, and practiced by almost every faith. Every religion speaks about the act of spending time in quiet contemplation, from the American Indians who go on vision quests, to the Buddhist monks in their monasteries, to the sect of the Jewish faith who spend quiet time in prayer facing a blank wall. Most faiths believe in the spiritual benefits of silence in solitude.

In addition, you can share with others at a retreat, just as I do at the Buddhist temple. There's a sense of unity and connectivity. You somehow get to know people on a soul level, rather than judging them by their physical appearance. I find that relationships are strengthened when you spend time away on a retreat, because you have the opportunity to distance yourself for a brief time — to clear away the unnecessary clutter and reconnect with what's essential. You'll often hear me saying, "There can't be a *we* until there's a *me*."

Give yourself and your soul the opportunity for a retreat. Don't just say, "Oh, yes, I really should try that sometime." Do it now, or else soon — you deserve it. It will improve your life, your health, and your attitude toward yourself and others. It will definitely help you approach your life from a more holistic perspective, inside and out. It truly is nourishment for your soul. Enjoy!

Reaching Out from Loneliness

How often have you found yourself sitting at home all alone on a Friday night after a hectic workweek? There's no phone ringing with invitations for dinner or offers to go for a walk in the country or to take in a movie. It's easy to slip into that familiar empty space of loneliness, but it's important that you refuse to give in to it so that it doesn't envelop you. If this typical scenario resonates with you, then I urge you to ask this question: "What am I going to do about it?"

I travel all over the world, meeting thousands of wonderful people during my lectures and demonstrations. I'm acutely aware of how easy it is to feel lonely. While traveling may seem romantic or exciting, it can also be an isolating experience. All people feel lonely at some point or other during their lifetime . . . it's a universal emotion. We not only experience it on a personal and emotional level, but we also feel it deep within our soul. We all need human contact and companionship — to be touched, be held, laugh, and share our feelings — so it's important to reach out to others. It's part of how we evolve, learn, grow, and mature as a human and as a soul.

I met a lively, outgoing woman who came to one of my workshops and told me about a successful business venture that she'd just sold. It was a novel idea, wherein a bunch of actors played the characters in an Italian wedding party. It was bit like going out for dinner and a movie, except in this case you *were* the movie!

Participants would pay to come and eat and join in with the actors as if they were guests at a real Italian wedding.

"People just love to dress up and go out," the woman explained. "They would party, dance, and toast the bride and groom. We had a full cast of characters who played everyone from the family to the newly married Italian couple." She said that everyone seemed to forget that they were at an improvisational wedding party and joined in to the hilt. Barriers were dropped and inhibitions left at home. She noticed how people who would normally be shy at social gatherings or reluctant to hug and kiss seemed to relish the warmth of being part of a crowd. She also told me about an elderly widow who came up to her to thank her for the evening. The woman said that it had been a long time since she'd been lovingly touched, and she expressed how good it felt to have a warm embrace from another human being. As the woman at my workshop and I said good-bye, I remember asking her if she realized when she came up with the idea just how therapeutic it would turn out to be.

All people deal with loneliness in their own way. Even my mom, who's been divorced for many years and lives alone, is considering volunteering at the local maternity ward because she loves taking care of babies. Newborn infants who are ill seem to recover much faster with regular human contact.

I want to stress that there's a major difference between being *alone* and being *lonely.* You could be alone in a remote cabin deep in the woods, hidden away from civilization, and still be at peace within yourself and your solitude. To understand *loneliness,* you have to recognize where it's coming from and what's causing it.

Many years ago, I used to work with a guy who was constantly telling me how lucky I was to be in a stable relationship and have someone to talk to. He was envious that I was seemingly never alone. Little did he know that it's possible to feel *more* lonely in a relationship than when you're single! I've heard this over the years from so many people. My co-worker didn't come from a loving background in a family who believed in touching or displaying outward signs of affection, so he grew up believing that people are generally distant and don't care about anyone except themselves. Is it any wonder that he ended up alone?

His sad upbringing was manifesting itself into loneliness. In his head, I'm sure that he was calling out for someone to touch him, hold him, and help him step out of his loneliness, but he made little attempt to reach out or heal, or even speak to a therapist. It was as though the past was keeping him frozen in his own personal coma. After some time, I finally realized that part of the cause was that he really didn't like himself. (If a person doesn't value who he is, then it's unlikely he's going to be comfortable alone with himself.) This man justified his solitude by convincing himself that people either didn't like him or didn't want to be around him.

In such a difficult situation, it's hard to know how to help those so firmly entrenched in their own despair. I encouraged him to reach out, but I got the same response every time: "What's the point?" I only wished that he could see himself from God's perspective, as a Divine, beautiful soul. I tried and tried to help him, but you can only do so much — and in the end, he moved away in an attempt to start over. I never heard from him again after that.

There are so many different forms of loneliness that can elicit pain. If you're by yourself, this condition may be self-imposed or the result of any number of causes. Every reason will be totally individual, and each solution will be unique. If you're suffering from loneliness, then do something about it now! Take the responsibility for reaching out to others. When you spend time being lonely and don't invest your energy in doing anything about it, you risk falling into a mind-set where you end up focusing on the negative — or worse still, you start beating yourself up. Equally, you can fall into a trap of blaming others for your loneliness.

Don't relive the past over and over again in your mind, as this is precisely how you'll attract what you're trying to avoid. There may be some emotional healing required before you begin to feel good about yourself, or if you've been let down or hurt in a personal relationship, you may need to learn to trust people again. If you're not used to being alone, you may have to acquire coping skills so that you *enjoy* being by yourself. There's so much support out there. Don't suffer alone: I urge you to reach out and ask for help. If you don't identify what may be causing your loneliness, it's easy to fill the void with less-healthy remedies, such as drugs, alcohol, bad relationships, or working all hours. None of these solve the problem — they're only a temporary solution.

I'm a big advocate of support groups for like-minded people where everyone shares in each other's story. The love from a small group can be amazing, whether you're lonely, you've lost your spouse, or you've been through a painful separation. We're all connected in this Universe and as a soul; we feel one another's pain. God put us here to share and to be with and assist one another. Remember that this goes back to serving your soul purpose of being all that you can be and helping humanity in a positive way.

Some Ideas to Help You with Loneliness

— **Journal out your feelings.** Journaling is a great way to let out all those inner feelings of being lonely, fearful, angry, or sad. It's *your* journal, with *your* feelings — no matter how much you may have suppressed them — so feel free to write whatever you want, without inhibition or restriction. When you journal out your emotions by putting pen to paper, you may see a pattern forming in your life, which enables you to take control and do something about it.

Journaling provides you with an opportunity to take a critical view of your own behavior, the causes of your loneliness, or how you react to others in a way that may push them away. When you write down your most intimate thoughts, you'll create a wonderful resource for the future. Over time, you'll be able to use your journals like an encyclopedia so that when a situation arises, you can take the best advice and guidance — in this case, your own. Your journals become a record of all the accomplishments and progress you've made. You can even write down particular blessings that are pertinent at the time or record what you're grateful for. When you're thankful for what you have, you create more abundance in other areas of your life. Journaling is a way to delve deep inside yourself to a place someone else may never reach, a place where you have the space to talk to your soul . . . it's always listening.

— **Do something totally different that you've never done before.** Break out of your day-to-day routine, and expand yourself beyond your comfort zone. No matter how safe it might feel to remain exactly where you are, it's important to occasionally stretch yourself. It could be a meditation or prayer group, salsa-dance lessons, a book club, an art class, or even a pottery workshop. Once, I took a cooking class at a local kitchen store just as a way of meeting some new people. Not only did I laugh and make some really interesting, diverse acquaintances, I also had a great time and learned how to prepare a new dish! I'm never going to be a gourmet chef, but that didn't matter.

So many people say, "But I hate going to those things alone!" or "How will taking a class help me?" When I went to this cooking class, *everyone* came by themselves. It was a way of reaching out and bonding with others in a safe, fun, and educational environment. If you're nervous about going somewhere alone, stop and say to yourself: *Wherever I go, there will be friends there.* It really works and takes the edge off those feelings of nervousness. Take a risk. You never know what's going to happen or whom you're going to meet and become friends with. Once again, it's a way of reaching out — at the very least, you're taking the first steps to do something about your solitude.

— **Connect with nature.** Nature has a wonderful way of healing and soothing your soul. Prana or chi (the life-giving energy from the Universe) is more bountiful outdoors. When you breathe it in, it clears your head; infuses you with positive, revitalizing energy; and provides a much-needed boost to your entire being. We're all energy, and everything from the smallest insect to the tallest tree — and even the blue sky — is made up of the same energy.

Try getting outside, whether it's for a walk on a beach or a hike in the woods. Appreciate the beauty that nature has to offer, whether you're gardening or choose to meditate in a serene area. God made this earth and blessed us with it, but it's so easy to get so caught up in life that you end up ignoring its beauty. I know people who live less than a mile from the most beautiful beach, yet they don't even visit it. I think they figure that it will always be there, but they hardly ever take the time out to enjoy it.

When you're outdoors, challenge yourself to do something physical. You may surprise yourself when you complete it, but notice the sense of achievement you feel inside. I've always had a great affinity for the ocean and wanted to try scuba diving, but I was really nervous the first time I took a class. When I made my first ocean dive, the sense of personal accomplishment I felt was amazing. My self-esteem and confidence got such a boost, and I remember walking back to my car feeling on top of the world. The whole experience left my soul singing. When you connect with nature — no matter what you choose to do or how far you choose to push yourself — you'll start to feel a complete connection to everything.

— **Volunteer your time.** Nothing makes you feel better than when you help another. The benefits work both ways, having a positive effect on you as well. I'm constantly in awe of people who freely volunteer. They seem to have ample amounts of compassion for others, as well as such tolerant and patient natures. When you volunteer your time, you develop a deeper understanding of the world, and the benefits can be wide-ranging, from enhanced inter-personal skills to improved coping abilities. My assistant's mom, who's 86, volunteers at the local homeless shelter serving food. She says that it gives her purpose, and she clearly relishes the joy of helping others who are less fortunate.

Animals also need our attention. Local shelters usually don't have a lot of money and need people to help out. In addition, volunteers who work in hospices (particularly those for children) are the unsung heroes, in my opinion. They admit that the spiritual and emotional compensation totally outweighs the time that they provide. Volunteers are the heart and soul of our society. I'm blessed with the opportunity to speak to thousands at my lectures, where I often say: "When you volunteer your time, you get bonus karma points in your favor!"

— **Become a leader within your community.** If you have a business or professional skill, I urge you to join a local neighborhood organization that would benefit from your expertise. Lori, a friend of mine, has a real passion for the arts. She volunteers her time and professional experience to the community art gallery, helping organize the art show every month and sitting on the board to ensure that the shows are well attended. Although she's relatively new to the area, she's quickly become a valued member of the community, always talking to someone new. Not only is she spreading and sharing the beauty and talent of the artists, she's nourishing her soul with the joy of helping others.

No matter what you do or how you work on your loneliness, the point is to do *something,* as long as you're moving in the right direction toward healing, liking yourself, trusting others, and learning to live a full life. No one else is responsible for your happiness . . . it's really up to you. When you begin to move beyond loneliness and understand that you're always connected to your soul — which in turn is connected directly to God, the Divine Source — you'll soon discover that you're never really alone, but are in fact connected to the whole Universe and everything in it.

Love Never Dies

Here's a scenario that everyone will be familiar with. You think of someone, you pick up the phone, you call, and the person who answers sounds somewhat surprised to hear your voice. You get the same response almost every time: "I was just thinking about you!" This is what I refer to as a "soul-to-soul" connection, although most people call it a form of telepathy. All thoughts are energy, and they travel through the ethers, whether out to the Universe or to those you may be thinking about.

It's the same mechanism for those on the Other Side when they want to communicate with you in this physical dimension. It's channeled by the power of love and thought, and it's this force that will always keep us connected to each other. How many times have you found yourself thinking about someone who's passed on? It's as though he or she just pops into your consciousness. This could be because at that *exact* moment, the person is lovingly thinking of you. Your loved ones are really just a thought away.

The veil between this world and the next is very thin. As a medium, I have the ability to see beyond that veil and communicate with the spirit world. As I make the connection, I always honor the souls' presence as I blend with their energy; and I get to see and feel them in their entirety — youthful, beaming, and luminous — even if it's for the briefest moment. I celebrate their joys and their sadness, as well as their love. It's such a privilege for me to do this work, but I've never considered it a job. The people who receive a message through me from loved ones on the Other Side often remark on what a beautiful gift they just received, but in reality, *I'm* the one who's received the ultimate gift: the chance for me to honor my soul purpose of being all that I can be as a spirit messenger helping others in their time of need.

Every time I demonstrate or work with a private client, I'm moved by the love from spirit for those still here on Earth. It's my belief that when you pass, your soul consciousness retains all your experiences and memories from this life. The entire history of your soul built up during your lifetime goes with you, as does the love for your friends and family. Those who are left behind often feel the caring emotion being sent from spirit as it touches their hearts and souls. The link works both ways: You can send your thoughts and love to people in the spirit world. We are, and always will be, connected to each other. Love is everlasting, and neither death nor time can separate us.

There are countless touching stories I've collected over the years, but one stands out in particular. It happened while I was working on an Alaska cruise. Several hundred people gathered for the afternoon lecture as the ship gently maneuvered away from the quay to head toward another port. I walked on the stage to greet a lively crowd and started to explain how I work.

"I'm going to raise my soul vibration, and those on the Other Side will lower theirs," I said. "It's a blending process as their energy merges with my aura. Once this happens, I'll be able to feel, see, or hear what the souls on the Other Side want to say." I went on to explain how they send feelings and messages and often validate the conditions of their passing. "They show me different scenes or symbols that I've learned to interpret. Sometimes they offer me precise words, songs, or even names. I'm even subjected to smells and tastes that are given to me," I told the audience. "It gets crowded up here. It's as though spirit is jockeying for the front row." This was my familiar introduction to the actual demonstration, as I knew that spirit would do anything to direct me to the right recipient.

I could feel the boat settle into a steady rhythm as I started the demonstration, and immediately, I found myself being pulled to the top row of the audience. Over my left shoulder, I heard a name that sounded like "Webster," and I pointed to the direction I believed it was intended for.

A very excited woman raised her hand and said, "I can understand the name Dempster, but not Webster." I explained the way I receive the sounds, how it could be fragmented and I have to try to sound out what I'm hearing. "Our last name is Dempster," she yelled out.

"Well, if this is for you, then you'll understand losing a child?" I inquired.

"Yes, yes!" the woman screamed. She was so excited that her enthusiasm was infectious and quickly spread through the audience.

When a child passes and the parents come to see me hoping for a connection, those are the readings that tug on my heartstrings more than most. The love between a parent and a child is one of the most precious and deep connections we make during our time here. Children start out as part of us, and from their first cries, they occupy a huge part of our hearts. We dream of watching them grow up to stand on their own and run free because it's the natural order of things. Of course a parent wants to leave this earth before his or her son or daughter makes that final journey. No one can explain why life doesn't cooperate and a child is inexplicably taken to the Other Side. When this happens, a parent is often left with more questions than answers, wondering, *Why did this happen? Is the Universe a fair place?*

The biggest concern for many parents is: "Who's taking care of my child now?" The fact is that no one wants to talk about the tragic death of a child for fear of adding to the suffering of the parents. That's why some mothers and fathers who've endured such a loss seek out a reputable medium to assist in their bereavement process. It's such a personal choice, one that should be taken seriously. I always encourage you to start with some grief counseling when you lose someone you've loved and cared for or have an unresolved issue with. Mediums are not the ultimate answer, as we can only assist you in the process.

The whole audience now turned to look at the woman and her husband, who was sitting next to her. I could feel the presence of her son Bruce so strongly as he stood beside me blending with my aura, which only increased the link. "I understand from what he's giving me that this is a very fast and tragic passing, and he didn't have the opportunity to say good-bye," I said.

By now, she was crying and holding her hands over her face. "Yes, it was tragic, and we didn't get to say good-bye to our son!" she sobbed.

"He isn't giving me how he passed and doesn't want you to remember him that way," I went on. "He's quite a happy boy, and I feel that he's a young man in his late teens or early 20s . . . would that be correct?" She was nodding in confirmation. I asked her for her name, and she introduced herself as Linda and her husband as Victor. I could feel Bruce's youthfulness and energy blending with my own, and I could barely contain myself from jumping up and down. He was clearly so excited to be there. As I started to talk, I knew that Bruce wanted me to mention his music, so I continued: "Would you understand him to be creative? He really wants me to talk about his music playing."

"Yes! Yes! Yes!" she shrieked, half out of her seat. Not only could I feel his love for his mother and father, but also the strength of Linda and Victor's love for their son. I was honored to be the special messenger for his parents on this day. However, he wasn't done and pushed me on.

"He's talking about you getting the tattoo for him."

"Yes! I had a tattoo done after he passed, and it's the exact duplicate of the one he had," she replied.

I could feel Bruce's laughter and joy as he had me tell her, "Please — no more tattoos, Ma!" At this point, her tears turned to laughter as she proudly told the audience that she'd had more than one done, and then she turned to me to ask if I wanted to see them. Heaven knows what she was about to show everyone!

"No, it's okay, Linda, as long as you understand the point of what he's trying to say: 'No more tattoos, Ma!'"

Bruce was keen to get back to his music, and he got me to mimic him playing his bass guitar. As soon as I started strumming my imaginary instrument, she screamed again as she verified that he was a bass player in a band and that his music had been his life. The entire audience was sharing in this special connection. They were smiling, crying, and laughing together. There were a lot of tissues getting handed out!

I could feel the link fading as he started to step back, and I said to Linda, "I know that I've mentioned the guitar, but before he leaves, he wants me to say something more about it. I feel that there's one more important thing about his guitar that I'm supposed to say."

Linda took a deep breath and looked at her husband with tears in her eyes, then turned to the audience: "John, we buried him with his beloved guitar!" There was an audible gasp, and for a second you could hear a pin drop.

Bruce knew that I had to give the evidence of his guitar for his parents to be certain that it was really him up there with me. I knew at that moment that the only other thing he loved as much as his parents was that guitar! He asked me to say one more thing to them: "Tell them I love them and I always will." With Bruce's personality and energy, I know that he must be rockin' 'n' rollin' in heaven.

Everyone was touched by his love. I told his parents afterward that not only were *they* affected by the message, so were all the people there — they'd taken away what they needed from it. Bruce's love had touched our hearts and our souls that day. I'm sure that when the audience members returned home at the end of the cruise, they took back the knowledge that love never dies . . . that it's everlasting, and that their loved ones are still connected to them and always will be.

Soul-to-Soul Connections

The soul is eternal, as it has no birth and never dies. It continues to exist long after the physical body experiences death, just as it did before entering the earthly realm. When loved ones leave this world, they embark on a journey as they return to the spirit world, their natural home. For those left behind, it's natural to grieve while working through the bereavement process. It can be hard to let go of the most recent memories of *how* they passed — how they looked, for instance, especially if they were very sick. Many people wonder what their loved ones were feeling just before they took their last breath.

As you reenter the spirit world, you arrive in your soul form, in perfect health once again. The same goes for your pets! All your illnesses and ailments are left behind with your physical body. I've frequently passed on messages from those who've recently departed, which are often similar. Usually all they want to confirm is that they're safe and they still love you. With death comes an interruption in the way we communicate with each other, and now a "new" way must be learned and used.

A healthy and helpful way to have your own soul connection with your loved ones (whether they're here or in the spirit world) is to make sure you know your own psyche. This means that you need to learn how to take control of your own thoughts, and more important, understand how they're sent and received on a psychic soul level. Husbands and wives or longtime partners are known to finish each other's sentences or utter the same words at exactly the same time. We all laugh when this happens and put it down to coincidence, but that's not always the case. How can you explain the way family members just know when there's something wrong? Why is it that when you think of people you haven't seen in a long time, you run into them or hear news about them?

These are not random coincidences. It's actually telepathy — or in other words, the ability to send and receive messages and information through the mind and soul. The energy of thought is a spiritual soul power, and I firmly believe that it's love that fuels this ability.

Even when I was linking with Bruce, I was speaking to him personally through the power of thought, as our souls and minds were linked and blended together during the communication. You're capable of this type of communication, too. Through the energy and the power of love, you're always connected with your family, friends, and pets both here and in the spirit world . . . it's a form of telepathic rapport.

You don't have to work with a medium to communicate with your loved ones who've passed over. In fact, it's true to say that you're receiving information secondhand when you use a medium (not that there's anything wrong with that). To experience your *own* connection, you have to be open to the whole idea of soul communication. As I said previously, if you suddenly find yourself thinking of them, or if their name suddenly comes up in a conversation, they could be sending you loving thoughts at the same time — it really does work both ways. Just be aware of each time you think of them, and keep an open mind. You should write in your journal to keep track of these communications, including when they happen and what you're doing at the time.

I heard a story that I related in my first book, *Born Knowing*. It tells of a little girl named Daisy and her belief in the power of thought. She passed away at the tender age of ten, but during her last days, Daisy often told her mother that she was communicating with her little brother who'd gone to the Other Side years earlier. In fact, Daisy explained to her mother that the little boy was standing right beside her, and the two were having quite a lively conversation. "How do you speak to your little brother? I don't hear or see you moving your lips," asked the bewildered mother. The little girl grinned as she answered: "We talk with our think, Mommy."

Another useful way to initiate communication is to find some of the happiest photographs of the person who's passed. If they were ill, don't imagine your loved ones as they looked in their final days; finding the most joyful pictures helps you remember them when they were vibrant and healthy. Spread the photos out and look into their eyes. Notice how the light behind them is coming from their soul. Close your eyes and just think of them. Reach out to them with your mind and with all the love you have in your heart.

The power of love between the two of you will keep you connected. You may see them in your mind's eye, sense a gentle brush against your skin, or feel their warm embrace as they wrap their arms and thoughts around you like a blanket where you feel safe and loved. They want you to be happy while you're here, and they desire that you go on until you meet them again in the spirit world. Keep the connection going by lovingly thinking of them. Reflect on and imagine them when they were *most alive* . . . because in reality, that's how they are now.

CHAPTER FIVE

The Healer Within

The ability to heal isn't restricted to those with some rare gift — we all have this capacity. Since our soul is the conduit for spirit (Divine Source), the power to heal flows within each and every one of us. This incredible force can be harnessed and used so that its energy enters our physical being to clear blockages, illnesses, past traumas, and emotional issues, as well as playing an important role in the process of forgiving. Healing energy can be accessed and utilized in many ways. The one thing to remember is to follow the natural spiritual law: *We're spirit in human form; and spirit is perfect and wants us to be whole in body, mind, and soul.*

The origin of the word *heal* is from the Anglo-Saxon word *hælen,* meaning "to be" or "to become whole." There's a significant difference between *healing* and *curing.* Although the dictionary offers a similar definition for both, it doesn't always suggest spiritual meanings. When I talk about *healing* (that is, self-healing), I'm referring to what's done *by* the person or the person's body in order to resolve a problem or issue concerning his or her body, mind, or soul. In contrast, the term *curing* usually refers to what's done *to* someone by a doctor or another health-care provider. *Curing* may treat the physical symptoms, and in cases where the diagnosis requires medical or surgical treatment, it's absolutely essential to follow that course of action. However, there's also the internal *healing* that you can initiate to assist you in removing or eliminating the underlying cause of the symptoms.

I highly recommend that you work with proper medical and health-care practitioners who know how to combine holistic and spiritual treatments. In partnership, they work so well to heal the *whole* you. When your body is trained to heal itself, you allow the powerful flow of energy to restore the natural balance of health and revitalize your zest for life!

A client of mine named Joan thoroughly understood the difference between healing and curing, but she was a habitual worrier. Her family members demanded a lot of her time so she could take care of their needs. She juggled a hectic schedule between her own life, work, and being the primary care provider for her parents. She worried *so* much that her physical body started to show signs of stress: She was only in her early 20s and was diagnosed with bleeding ulcers. Medication certainly went some way toward reducing the discomfort, but it couldn't treat the cause, so the pains in her stomach frequently recurred. She'd come in to get a reading for a totally different reason, but this issue quickly raised its head, as it was occupying such a large part of Joan's consciousness.

I felt that I really needed to help her learn some basic techniques to calm and relax her body as well as her mind. Worry can be a crippling disease if it's not checked early and dealt with. It eats away at the soul, thus depleting the vital energy that sustains us. It was only when Joan started some serious soul-searching regarding her responsibility toward herself and her family that the true healing process began. She knew that she had to heal the cause, rather than continually masking the symptoms.

So much *dis-ease* comes from our own self-inflicted condition arising from how we think, eat, feel, speak, and act. This usually originates in negative and often traumatic emotional experiences from the past, or in some cases, ones that are happening right now. Such experiences promote negative thought patterns, which if left unchecked, can easily turn into an illness. These conditions could have been set in motion in our formative years as a child, so we're not always to blame. However, I believe that we have the choice as to how we handle and treat that negativity.

To start any healing process, you have to let go of any old, limiting beliefs in your mind as well as your soul. Begin healing the *whole* you by changing your own attitudes, perceptions, and behaviors. As you learn to work on your soul-self, you'll identify and peel away the layers of your limitations, enabling you to finally let them go.

As a medium, I've witnessed healings on both a physical and spiritual level. During my intensive training as a medium in the U.K., I studied various forms, one being a mode of spiritual healing. In many of the spiritualist churches there, accredited healers are available who devote time to those who need their help during the church service. I noticed that there were some common qualities that each healer possessed, such as generosity, compassion, and above all, love.

Love is seen as one of the most important motivating factors for the power to heal. Why is this emotion so important when we talk about healing? As humans, we should regard it as the most significant element in our lives. Loving ourselves as well as others can be a powerful force. It comes from the deepest part of us and is part of our true essence.

During the sessions that I witnessed, the healer would often stand silently behind the people as they arranged their chairs in a neat circle. The atmosphere was calm — almost serene — and the energy of love flowing through the church was amazing. I sat and observed in silence, although there were many times when I had to muffle a gasp. I witnessed images and lights that seemed to appear around the healers, and my heart was full because I was so grateful for the guidance and education that I was gaining simply by watching them.

"May I place my hand on your shoulders and send you healing?" one healer asked a man with crippling back pain, whose suffering was clearly etched on his face. I watched as they both closed their eyes. It was an extraordinary sight: The man's face began to relax as if his excruciating pain dissipated. Although it only lasted a few minutes, I could almost see the power of spirit flowing through the healer into this man. Tears began to run down his face, and the discomfort in his back eased to such an extent that he left the service walking considerably straighter.

There's another form of healing that some mediums practice called *absent healing*. Spiritual energy, combined with healing thoughts, can be sent to a patient miles away. There are no boundaries when it comes to sending healing energies of love and compassion.

I've seen many mediums practicing different forms of healing, including spiritual healing, Reiki, Pranic Healing, hands-on healing, qigong, Therapeutic Touch, as well as tai chi. One thing is perfectly clear: Energy doesn't come *from* the healers, but *through* them. The role of a healer is to help patients attune themselves to their *own* natural healing capacity. Edgar Cayce once said: "Spirit is seen as the God Force abundantly manifesting in the human body." He also stated: "True healing can be accomplished only when the spiritual nature of the human being is recognized as Divine." Never was a truer word spoken.

No healer can, or should, guarantee a cure. If you come across such claims, then I urge some caution. For a successful healing to take place, there's a set of conditions that all reputable healers abide by. For example, they need to be in good health themselves, both in body and mind. Equally, there might be a karmic condition that could affect the outcome for the recipient. Healings don't always take effect immediately, and the full benefits can be felt over time. Remember that we're powerful beings and capable of miracles. When it comes down to it, we know that we have to let go — and let God.

The following sections will provide you with some techniques to harness the incredible healing ability that's within you and use it on both yourself and others.

Body-Mind-Soul Connection

Do you know how much of a miracle you truly are? The Source that makes all living things in the Universe is the same one that's inside of you. This Divine Source interacts and is connected with the *whole* of you, which means your body, mind, and soul. Everyone at one time or another has experienced what's known as the *body-mind-soul connection.*

Throughout my spiritual development, I've always been fascinated by the power and capability of the mind. I studied the body-
mind connection when I was training to be a certified hypnothera-
pist. As I practiced the rudimentary mechanics of hypnosis, I began
to understand that the brain and body *do not* differentiate between
sensory images from the mind as opposed to those in reality. It's
been well documented that the chemical activity that takes place
during visualizations and hypnosis is in fact the same as when we
experience reality with our own physical senses.

A person could put an ice cube on the skin of someone under
hypnosis and suggest that it's a hot coal. The skin would react as if
it were burning. Try this: Imagine that a piece of lemon is in front
of you and see if you start to salivate. By the same token, if you
smell an apple pie, it can trigger sweet memories from the past,
or you might hear a certain song that tugs at your heartstrings.
When you have a strong image, it's usually followed by a powerful
response. This is absolute proof of the body-mind connection.

It's easier for doctors to treat the physical issues than to diag-
nose what's going on in your emotional and spiritual body. When
I talk about "body" in this case, I'm referring to the different auric
energy bodies that surround you. Your body records *everything*,
and you store these memories on a cellular level from the moment
you're born. When you first become aware of a particular symptom,
it can also be a sign for you to pay attention to what's happening
in a certain area of your life. In order for healing to begin, you have
to consider integrating all of your experience — in other words, the
totality of your body, mind, and soul.

Doctors usually treat physical symptoms but don't always get
to see the bigger picture. Years ago, our regular doctor knew our
family and its history and was our physician for life, but with the
evolution of medical practices and the health-insurance industry,
we've become more accustomed to visiting a hospital or clinic with
multiple doctors. Often we're in and out in less than 30 minutes.
Next! Hopefully, we use all the expertise offered by medical science
in conjunction with our own internal soul resource for healing.

Earlier I talked about the powerful effects that are generated
through visualization. When you picture yourself happy, healthy,

and whole, the chemicals and electrical activity in your body begin to react and respond. Your body believes what it's seeing — so now you know why the phrase "Think positive" is so popular: Having an upbeat attitude *does* work. It can actually reduce healing time, and I've heard of people experiencing fewer complications after surgery when they approached recovery with a positive outlook. Above all, it leads to an overall balance as you allow your body, mind, and soul to work together in harmony.

I see many people at the gym using visualization techniques in their exercise programs as they tap into the body-mind connection. They imagine how they want to look, the muscles that they need to tone and define, and the fitness goals that they'd like to accomplish. They begin to feel the emotion of their physical aspirations being manifested. Athletes and their coaches are now using the practice of body-mind connection through visualization to enhance performance. Doctors, too, are starting to appreciate its benefits, and mind-body therapeutic techniques are currently being studied and taught at medical schools all over the world. Even the wonderful healing power of laughter is now being harnessed as humor therapy and different forms of comic relief are becoming part of some patients' rehabilitation programs. Emotions can create dis-ease, which can cause a disruption in the balance of life, but on the positive side, they can act as a healing agent to put life back on course again.

Start planting new seeds of healing and wellness today. There are many useful techniques that you can learn, including meditation, guided imagery, relaxation, prayer, self-hypnosis, and group therapy. If you're practicing the "Relaxing the Body" meditation that I gave you in Chapter 3, then you're already on your way. Here's another exercise that's almost identical and will continue to assist you in getting to know your physical vehicle, or as I refer to it, the *temple of your soul.* As always, I suggest that you keep track of your self-work, experiences, and progress in your journal.

EXERCISE: Connecting to Your Body

This is a simple exercise that will help you relax. It's designed to increase your body awareness. So before we begin, let's get comfortable. . . .

Make sure that you're wearing loose-fitting clothing. Sit comfortably in a straight-back chair, with your feet flat on the ground and your hands resting on your lap. For this exercise, it's better to be sitting rather than lying down, as I don't want you falling asleep. It's important for you to be relaxed, but it's also essential that you're comfortably alert and aware during the meditation.

Now close your eyes and breathe in slowly, then gently exhale all that tension. Once again, breathe. Gently move all the parts of your body as you settle into a relaxed state. Try to become aware of your left foot, and slowly focus your attention there, tensing and relaxing that area. Gradually move your attention up your left leg and notice if there's any tightness in this region. If so, raise your left leg and try tensing the muscles, then release them and relax. Maintain the steady breathing rhythm as you slowly move your awareness up your left side, into your abdominal area, up to your chest, to your shoulder, and then down your left arm all the way to your fingers. Clench your left hand into a fist, and then relax it.

Now, moving in the reverse direction, shift your awareness up your arm again to your shoulder, down your neck, and all the way down your back. As before, if you feel strain, just tense the muscles, slowly release, and relax — then move on. Good, now slowly move your awareness up to your head, scalp, and face and let go of any tightness in your jaw. Release any tension and feel the sense of relaxation wash over you.

Once you've worked up the left side, do the same for the right, but this time start from the head, then move down your right shoulder, arm, hand, thigh, calf, foot, and to your toes. Let your awareness slowly scan your whole body and see if there's one place that's calling out for attention. Always release the tension and relax.

Try to notice if there's still any residual tightness left over in a certain area, and if so, tense and gently release. It may be stubborn, so you might want to ask your body if that certain spot is holding on to a past memory or an emotion that needs to be released. Try to notice the particular body part that requires more effort to relax. There's no need to rush — spend a moment with that area and let the healing relaxation begin to move through it and on to the rest of the body. Take as much time as you need. Simply notice what it feels like to be connected to your entire body. When you're ready, slowly open your eyes and begin to move your toes, legs, fingers, and arms.

You and your body have just begun a new partnership with each other, a resourceful and intuitive alliance that can grow and get stronger as you become more connected to each other.

Your body has a way of sending you signals through its own intuitive language. Whether it's a gut response, a physical sensation, an emotion, or even a dream — your body is talking to you! We generally don't pay enough attention to it or heed its signals until something goes wrong. If you hear a ping, rattle, or whine in your car, hopefully you'd head straight down to the nearest garage without hesitation. So all I'm asking is that you treat your body with the same respect. During the process of spiritual development, don't push those physical sensations or your feelings away. Embrace them and listen to them. Often through meditation, you'll be able to find the answer to what your body is trying to say — so just ask. You may not get anything at first, but it's worth persevering, as it really does get easier with practice.

The Healing Power of Prayer

In today's world of technological advances and medical breakthroughs, many people question the validity of the power of prayer to heal — but it has been definitively shown to assist in healing. A survey of 31,000 adults, released in 2004 by the National Center for Health Statistics, found that 43 percent of U.S. adults prayed for their own health, while 24 percent had others pray for it. I think that those figures speak for themselves.

Research has been undertaken exploring the positive effects of prayer. An article published in the *Annals of Internal Medicine* in

2000 reported on 23 studies of various distant-healing techniques including religious, energy, and spiritual healing. One investigation, conducted between 1982 and 1983, drew a lot of attention. Some 393 patients in the San Francisco General Hospital's coronary care unit participated in a double-blind study to assess the therapeutic healing effects of prayer. One group was prayed for, while the others were not. As I firmly believe in the power of prayer, I wasn't surprised by the results of the study: The participating patients who were prayed for had fewer CPRs (cardiopulmonary resuscitations) performed and were less dependent on life-support systems and medicine. Of all the results, though, the most remarkable was that there were fewer deaths among those patients.

Another study, conducted by Dr. Franklin Loehr, a minister and scientist, proved that seeds that were prayed over produced quicker germination and healthier plants. Those that were *not* prayed over had stunted growth, and in some plants, germination didn't even take place. The experiment was repeated several times with the same result.

Hopefully, in the future more and more studies will be carried out to show how the power of prayer can help with the healing of others and ourselves, not just in the body, but in the mind and soul as well. It doesn't matter which faith or religion we follow, as we all can tap into the universal Source that sustains us.

Exactly what is prayer? Prayer (whether spoken or unspoken) is communicating with God, a higher power, the Universe, or what I refer to as the Divine Source. Simply put, when you pray, you connect. It's a way for us as human beings to become involved and develop a relationship with the Source. This connection can benefit our lives on so many more levels than just healing.

Most religions agree that there's one true Source that cares about you, no matter who you are or what your personal circumstances. It wants to respond to you and your needs, but It wants you to respond back — there has to be a two-way communication, since It hopes so very much to help you. Even if you don't fully believe in a supreme deity or follow a certain faith, there may be times when you find yourself offering a small prayer of gratitude, whether or not you're totally aware of who you're thanking.

Praying enables you to forge a relationship with something that you may not be able to see but which is truly there.

When I pray, I ask to be merged with the Divine Source and to feel Its presence in my heart. You may pray by repeating positive affirmations. The repetitive rhythm gives them strength and power — it's like a form of chanting. In many cultures and civilizations, chanting is a way of seeking greater health, a sense of well-being, enlightenment, and a connection to the Divine. This activity unites and infuses the mind, body, and soul through the breath. You can write your own chants using names, words, sounds, syllables, or even sections of text. It's not so much about *what* you chant, but more about your willingness to commit to the act of chanting, which lets you raise your own vibrations to a higher spiritual level. The benefits are extraordinary as the surge of energy permeates your body, and the feeling of pure joy fills your heart.

The Native Americans use drumming and chanting as a form of prayer in their ceremonies. Other groups sing out their prayers in music and song, while some repeat their requests using the rosary. Buddhists also use prayer beads, and some commune with God through meditation. No matter what style of praying you choose, it's important for you to begin. Don't worry how you practice it at first or for how long. Don't get caught up in trying to find the right words or the correct prayer intentions — God won't be upset with you, even if you don't have much to say. Just pray, give thanks, and begin to commune with the Divine Source. This is your time to express your concerns and whatever you're feeling and experiencing in your life. Through prayer, the Source will reach out to your consciousness, your mind, and your soul. It wants your love . . . after all, *love* is the highest form of praise.

I know that life presents many obstacles and challenges, but far too many people only pray when they want God to help them with their problems. Try not to pray *just* when you desire something, but rather, take the time to do so to give praise and gratitude. Pray when you're at peace. Pray because you want to. Pray to just say hello to God. Pray to help you understand how prayer works. Pray for the simple act of praying.

As you practice this art, you'll begin to see your life in a different way. You'll find that you welcome in new, vibrant people and experience a renewed sense of inner confidence, knowing that your prayers are being heard and answered. Don't just sit and wait for a response to your prayers . . . think back on how some of them might have been answered in the past. We don't always get what we want, but we usually get what we need. Begin noticing *how* your prayer requests are being fulfilled. Have you been given a new book that has somehow revealed the answer you were praying for? Has a complete stranger recently come into your life and provided you with wonderful guidance? Is synchronicity taking you by the hand and leading you to find a resolution? Now you may understand the meaning of the saying "God moves in mysterious ways" a little better. Simply pray, and don't expect the answer to necessarily show up in the way that you think it should arrive — just give thanks when it does.

This reminds me of a beautiful story. A man was a bit concerned because he heard that there was a storm coming in the direction of his village and that it would rain for many days. He had faith in God and said to himself, *Have no worry; God will provide.* Well, the storm came as predicted, with day after day of torrential rain. The village started to flood, and the water was lapping at his window, yet he said to himself, *Don't worry; God will provide.* That day, some people from the village came by looking for those who needed assistance. They offered to help move the man and carry his belongings to safer ground. He waved at them kindly and said, "No, thank you; God will provide."

The rain continued, and the next day some men came in a small boat and called out to the man: "Come on! The rain isn't stopping, and the water is continuing to rise! The village is being evacuated — get some of your belongings, and we'll take you to safety in our boat." The man refused again, saying, "No worries; God will provide."

After several days, the water was now up to the man's roof. He climbed onto it, and as he did so, a helicopter came by and the pilot yelled out on the loudspeaker: "I'll send down the lift. Get in it, and I'll take you to safety." The man of course waved to the pilot and yelled back, "No, thank you, sir; God will provide!"

When the water covered his whole house, he was left sitting on the chimney. He held his head high and looked up as he screamed to God: "I've prayed and prayed to You, so why have You forsaken me?" At that exact moment, a booming voice answered him: "Forsaken you?! Who do you think sent the townspeople, the men in the boat, and the helicopter?"

When you begin, it's okay to make up your own little prayers before you jump into a novena. Keep them short and simple. A good one to start off with as soon as you wake up in the morning is: "I love You. Please bring me Your blessings for my highest good." It may sound elementary, but it's powerful. Say it a few times during the day and before you go to sleep . . . keep repeating it. You may also decide to add in your own affirmations — for example: "I am now following my soul's purpose, and God is bringing the right people into my life," or even, "With God in my corner, I can achieve anything!"

Mix the prayers up and personalize them as much as possible. Record them in your journal as they change and evolve. Over time, you can spend more time in prayer as you experiment to see what form you're comfortable with. Remember that God — the Universe, the Divine Source — doesn't care how you pray as long as you do so from your heart and soul. You'll develop a loving relationship wherein the Source and your soul connect in spiritual union, bringing you blessings of comfort, inspiration, and strength that could take you through the rest of your life.

I'd like to leave you with a prayer that has a special meaning for me and brings me comfort and peace when I repeat it several times. I hope that it helps you during any difficult times, so you too can benefit from its wisdom.

Serenity Prayer

God grant me the Serenity to accept the things I cannot change,
Courage to change the things I can,
and the Wisdom to know the difference.

Soul Energy

In order to lead a completely soul-filled, energetic life, giving life everything that you have to offer and being all that you can be, you must have your soul power entirely intact. I've said before that we're all made up of energy — as energetic beings, we have what are known as *energy cords,* which we constantly emanate, whether consciously or unconsciously. When you direct your thoughts and energy to a particular person, place, object, situation, or even an uncompleted project, you begin to establish an energetic cord with whatever you're focusing on. The more you send your power there or obsess about it, the bigger and stronger the cord becomes. In turn, what happens is that your energy attaches itself to the object of your concern, and your own precious resource seeps away from your soul, where it's most needed.

I'm sure that you've heard the expression "giving your power away." Well, that's exactly what happens. Not only are you giving it away, creating a soul leakage, but you also become energetically involved once this energy connection has been established. I'm not advocating that you never become attached or that you disconnect yourself from those around you or from life itself. You *can* have healthy attachments to people, places, and situations, ones that feed your soul and supply you with energy. Rather, I'm referring to *anything* that's taking your power away and draining you — the unforeseen connections that pull or tug on your energy, leaving you feeling sucked dry.

Not long ago, a client named Kathy came to see me. On a psychic level, I immediately saw the phenomenal potential that she possessed. She had the power to manifest whatever she wanted in her life, but here's the catch: Although she had all the makings of someone who achieves great things, she was unable to overcome the obstacles she faced and fulfill her potential. Kathy had issues at work, worried about her family, and was embarking on a new relationship all at the same time. In addition, there was a plethora of projects around the house that she'd started but hadn't finished — and to cap it all off, she had major financial obligations. Even though she was healthy, she constantly suffered from a lack of energy; as a result, nothing was really getting completed. She'd seen her doctor and undergone all the proper tests, but they couldn't find anything physically wrong.

After speaking with her for a while, I told her that she was an energetic being, and her energy — or in other words, her soul force — was leaking away from her. In order for her to live a healthy life, she needed to start cutting the cords with some of the things that were draining her reserves. It was vital to reclaim the power that was meant for her, to recharge her physical battery (her body) as well as her soul.

We talked for a while about all her cords, and I could see that she quickly understood what needed to be done. She wrote to me months later to say that she'd joined an Al-Anon group to help deal with family issues, had quit her mundane job, found another job that inspired her, hired an accountant to handle her finances, and was devoting quality time to herself and to her new relationship. By facing up to the situations that were draining her energy and by cutting those cords, she now had more than enough energy. Her health improved, and she was able to say, "I feel passionately alive and whole again. I am now stepping into my power!" She even had time to take up a new hobby that she'd always wanted to try, one that would feed her soul — ballroom dancing!

Remember in the first chapter when I talked about imagining yourself as an automobile? The outside of the car is your physical body, the driver is your soul, and the fuel that runs the vehicle is spirit infusing your soul to enable you to move steadily forward. Well, since you're the vehicle, just be aware of how many of those energy cords you're sending out and attaching to things so that you don't end up running on empty. Make sure that you're living a balanced and healthy lifestyle — after all, you're a soul manifested in physical form. Are you getting proper rest and exercise? Are you eating well and consuming all your supplements and the vitamins that your body needs? These things add energy to your system, rather than taking it away.

Take out your journal and make a list of whatever (or *who*ever) is draining, irritating, or upsetting you — or even issues you may be unclear about. These could be in *any* area, including your personal, work, and home life. Break down the list into categories, and go through them one by one. Making this list is an important step. You'll start noticing where your energy is going, and you'll be able to make decisions that are more informed when you want to cut the cord and deal with it. It's amazing when you start this process: You'll get your energy back, and in so doing, you'll begin healing all of you.

Here are a few examples of potential draining energy cords:

- Family concerns
- Unhealthy diet
- Lack of exercise
- Putting off a health checkup
- Relationship issues that have never been addressed
- Uncompleted projects (personal, home, or work)
- Unresolved financial issues
- Excessive worrying
- Taking on the problems of a friend

Give life your *best,* and do things that you feel passionate about instead of just talking about them. Remember that your body acts like one big psychic antenna, receiving energy, thoughts, and feelings — and the same metaphor applies when you're sending out energy. Anytime you're feeling drained or tired, you can tap into the Divine Source to obtain as much energy as your body needs. Many of the exercises and techniques throughout this book will enable you to be open and receptive to this Divine energy, letting it flow into your system.

Now it's time to get your energy moving in the right direction and take a long, hard look at your life. When you're interacting with the different people in it, are they giving you energy, or are they taking it away? Is there an even exchange? There should be a balance of giving and receiving. I want you to become more consciously aware of when and where you give away your power — the power that infuses your soul and that's meant for you. Honor it.

The Healing Power of Forgiveness

The act of forgiveness is incredibly powerful in its own right — it has the capacity to heal and transform. I'm sure you've heard the expression "Forgive and forget," but don't dismiss it too quickly. Many of us still try to forget, push away, or not think about some hurt that was done to us in the past. We live in the hope that our heart will heal on its own, and any bad feelings will just fade away. Sadly, this approach doesn't always work. By holding on to anger or resentment toward others as well as ourselves, the emotions begin to worsen on a vibrational or energetic level.

If you've been hurt in the past and are hanging on to negative feelings, they can take their toll on your physical, mental, emotional, and spiritual well-being. Psychological effects include depression, tension, anxiety, and stress. In addition, your cardiovascular, digestive, muscular, and nervous systems can all be affected.

Some people hold on to these feelings for weeks, months, years, or in the most severe cases, for the rest of their lives. People usually have to blame someone. In this situation, they become accustomed to a life filled with rage, hurt, anger, and bitterness. They assume the personality of that energy, and the negative emotions *become* who they are. If all those feelings were removed, who would they be?

Since we're energy, we end up holding on to these emotions of pain and anger. We resonate specific vibrations by the natural laws of "like attracts like." We end up attracting others who have the same issues and problems. This is another example of energy drain, which I call *soul leakage*. For many of us, it's impossible to imagine forgiving someone who's caused such physical, mental, or emotional pain — especially when the hurt is deep. Making the conscious decision to do so and letting go of the suffering is the beginning of the healing process. When we forgive, we can get back to cherishing ourselves and start to vibrate at a higher level through our heart center, attracting love. Now wouldn't you rather be drawing that into your life instead of pain and negativity?

We've all been hurt at some point or another, but many of us keep letting the same people do it over and over. It's a vicious circle: If someone perpetually hurts you, it's likely that it will result in a habit of negative behavior, which is replayed and relived over and over again in your head as well as your heart. You have to break the unhealthy cycle. If you can't find it in your heart to forgive, you risk long-term suffering and create conflict with your true soul-self.

I believe that people think that they're protecting themselves somehow by not practicing forgiveness. You could very well be blocking your soul's path and the evolution to new spiritual life experiences and opportunities. When you begin to practice forgiveness, don't be surprised if old wounds and memories, as well as sad and negative feelings, emerge. It's necessary for them to resurface from their hiding places so that you can start the healing process.

Forgiveness is all about choice. It doesn't necessarily mean releasing people from responsibility for their actions — it's a matter of releasing the anguish that *your* soul is carrying around with it. Whether or not others deserve to be forgiven, just remember that you're doing it for yourself. Forgiveness enables you to use your energy in a healthier and more productive way. Each time you practice it, you have the potential to break the cycle of pain. When you express true forgiveness, you empower yourself to stop feeling like a victim. You begin to let go of any feelings that you were wronged, and your capacity to love and trust is enriched as those emotions of hurt and anger melt away.

In the deepest part of your heart and soul, you have the ultimate power to heal, move past issues that have been holding you back, and live a life of total freedom. There's a quote that I came across (although the author is unknown) that states: "To forgive is to set a prisoner free and discover that the prisoner was you."

I'm often asked questions such as: "How do I move on so that I can get back and enjoy my life again?" Some years ago, a client told me a disturbing story. Helen was a giving and warmhearted soul who often helped her friends in any way she could with the little time she had in her schedule. She was a high achiever and was the sort of person who got things done efficiently and quickly, which meant that people noticed her.

She'd become close to a work colleague and had confided in her, telling her some personal details, along with a few of her plans for the future. They quickly forged a warm friendship based on what appeared to be mutual interests and beliefs. One day, however, she got a phone call from another friend who was clearly embarrassed when she told Helen that her new confidant was saying negative, hurtful things about her behind her back. This supposed friend was making derogatory statements about her being too arrogant and bigheaded. It was ridiculous!

Helen was upset and wondered why this woman would say such things. Her mind began to race as she asked herself, *What have I done to her to deserve such treatment? How could she do this? Should I call or not call her?* Helen's immediate response was to pick up the phone and scream back at the woman, but she resisted. She had to stop for a minute and create a more positive mind-set again. She'd allowed all of the unkind comments to consciously weaken her confidence and erode her self-esteem. It was as if she suddenly became immersed in negative self-talk. This woman had somehow burrowed into her subconscious, and as a result, Helen had internalized the negative thoughts, which were altering the way she was seeing herself and her reality. Before she could take any action, she had to rebuild her confidence, so she set about doing so by feeding her mind with positive, empowering thoughts.

As the fog lifted, Helen started to see what was truly going on. She made some discreet inquiries, and to her surprise, she found out that her colleague had quite a reputation for bad-mouthing other people. The more she found out about her, the clearer it all became: The woman was apparently riddled with jealousy, blaming others for her own shortcomings. In this case, my client made the decision to forgive her — to let it go, since it really wasn't a personal attack on her; it was more about the other person. Helen broke the energetic cord with the woman, and the pain quickly subsided. Now the incident is only a distant memory to her — just like the friendship.

As part of the process of severing emotional cords in the future, I taught Helen a simple yet empowering mantra to help her with forgiveness and moving on with her life: *Dealt with it — Done with it — Empowered by it!* I also left her with one of my famous quotes, attributed to Eleanor Roosevelt: "Great minds discuss ideas; average minds discuss events; small minds discuss people." I love that one!

To begin the practice of forgiveness, you must let go of the negative emotions within yourself that are holding you prisoner, preventing you from living a healthy, soul-filled life. You can use your motivated mind-set to encourage yourself by changing your approach and outlook. If you're hesitant about forgiving, you can always spend some quiet time alone and focus on positive self-talk to convince yourself that it's worth your while to forgive. Be open to receiving guidance or assistance from others. Many therapists, coaches, and counselors recommend that their patients make a list of the people in their lives who need forgiveness (even if they've passed away).

Imagine yourself in a safe, comfortable place — maybe a special location that means something just to you. In your mind, visualize the person whom you want to forgive walking up to you. Really see him or her, but try not to reconnect with the feelings of anger, resentment, or pain that this individual may have caused you — this exercise is about letting go of these emotions . . . it's about cutting the cord and moving on. Take a slow, deep breath and imagine that you're both surrounded by a beautiful shade of green light emanating from the heart. The light's healing properties help you forgive, as they ease the hurt and the emotions from the past.

If you try this for yourself, it's helpful to say your own positive healing affirmations. Here are a few of my favorites:

I now bring in the healing power of forgiveness.
I now forgive you and release you.
I release myself from the emotions of the past.
I forgive myself for accepting the belief pattern of pain and suffering.
My heart is now open to receive love in my life.

When you try this, don't be alarmed if it takes days, weeks, or even longer to become aware of the feelings of forgiveness. You may have been holding on to issues for quite some time, so give yourself as long as it takes. You'll know when it's *complete*, because you'll begin to feel a positive shift — it's like a huge weight is lifted. You'll feel physically lighter, since you're no longer held prisoner by the past. Forgiveness doesn't have to be asked for, bought, traded, or earned . . . it's a gift for you. The gift that comes from forgiveness is love.

Forgiving Yourself

Do you find it easier to forgive others than yourself? There may be times when you do something that you're not proud about. Yes, we all act like this from time to time — some of us more often than others! The feelings of shame and guilt will complicate your life, causing stress and emotional discord that will weigh heavily on your soul.

Societal conditioning encourages us to forgive others for their actions, but if we don't do the same for ourselves, we'll end up holding the key to our own prison. Many of us agonize over our past mistakes, living them over and over again in our minds, like a video player caught in a perpetual replay loop. It depletes our energy and prevents us from forgiving ourselves.

When you feel guilty, you attract punishment into your life; and in situations that are more serious, you even manifest it for yourself. It's easy to reconcile the feelings by saying, "I deserve this." Early in this chapter, I wrote out the Serenity Prayer, and there's part of it that I want to repeat: "God grant me the Serenity to accept the things I cannot change, [and] Courage to change the things I can." Your past mistakes may not be fixable, but you can acknowledge, accept, and take responsibility for them and begin the healing process within yourself.

If you've hurt someone and need closure about those feelings, maybe it's time to be courageous. Talk to the person and really *listen* with an open heart to the explanation of how he or she has been hurt by you. Don't go on the defensive — just listen. Understand how he or she feels. Try to apologize, but if the person is reluctant to accept your apology, then acknowledge the pain that you've caused. Remember that it's often just as important for the other person to come to terms with the hurt, to understand the whys and wherefores, since this individual needs closure, too.

Equally, you may want to ask forgiveness of someone who's passed away. When I link with spirit as a medium, I often connect with souls who look back at their lives and the people still on the earthly plane with a new sense of wisdom, appreciation, and understanding. I'm sure that they don't take past grudges across with them. There are times when I feel their forgiveness so strongly in our link.

Every time you make amends for the wrongs you've done to others, you begin the healing journey — for them as well as yourself. It may take some time to regain their trust or respect. Ask them what they expect of you and what you can do for them, or be more proactive and offer up a few suggestions. On a soul level, it's worth it.

I want to remind you again that you're a spiritual being in human form and you experience everything in the physical world, but as a human, you make mistakes. It's only natural that you'll continue to commit more errors in this lifetime and your future ones after that. As long as you're learning from past mistakes and moving in a positive direction, you'll be living and loving from your soul as well as your heart.

EXERCISE: Self-Forgiveness

Close your eyes and take a deep, cleansing breath. With each inhalation, feel the love of spirit, the Divine Source, coming into your being. Sense it slowly and gently wrap itself around your whole body. Accept this loving energy. Now picture in your mind's eye an image of yourself at the age when you were most vulnerable. Really see yourself, and look deep into your eyes. You know that *the eyes are the windows of the soul,* and they somehow seem to be asking, *Will you forgive me?*

Be aware, and acknowledge that you're taking responsibility for hurting another or yourself. Now let this energy fill your entire heart area. Hold it there for a moment, and say: "Dear [your name], I hold you in my heart with all this love and want the very best for you in this moment. I love you and forgive you for the painful choices and mistakes that you have made in the past. I now release and let go of the experience with love."

The Healing Breath

You have access to an incredible resource that's available 24/7, but the best part is that it's absolutely free! Used to its full potential, it can have a significant and positive effect on your well-being, acting as a channel to show you how powerful you are as a soul. You can tap into it by simply *taking your next breath.* When you enter this world, the *first* thing you do is inhale, and before you leave this life, the *last* thing you do is exhale. Life is therefore one continuous series of breaths.

As I became more spiritually aware, I was fascinated by the mechanics of my own psychic abilities. I found myself drawn to the Eastern traditions and spent many a long afternoon reading and studying. As a result, I quickly appreciated the value and significance of working with the breath. The philosophy is based on the principle that *breath is life,* and that it's the bridge between your body and soul. Eastern teachers have thankfully passed on their beliefs and techniques to many of us in the West. We've learned that in addition to the obvious physical benefits derived from proper breathing techniques, these practices also increase our mental agility, happiness, and willpower.

You're often barely aware that you breathe, taking this miracle for granted. Once the breath becomes part of your everyday awareness, you'll wonder how you survived before you started paying attention to it. After all, it affects everything you do.

Ancient Eastern and Western spiritual philosophies teach us about the universal life force that runs through everything, including *you*. This spiritual energy breathes life into your body and keeps you connected to the universal force that surrounds you. (If you're interested in furthering your knowledge of the breath, I highly recommend a wonderful educational guide called *Science of Breath*, by Yogi Ramacharaka.)

Ancient Chinese medicine has its own unique name for this universal energy that flows through us, referring to it as *chi* — the Hindus call it *prana*. It surges through our vital organs, permeates our bones, and revitalizes our bloodstream and other parts of the body along a network of internal systems called *meridians*. This spiritual energy is what healers and other natural-health practitioners (such as acupuncturists, reflexologists, energy healers, and some massage therapists) work with in the process of removing blockages in our energy system. When ignored, these blockages can manifest themselves in the body as ailments and aches and pains; or left untreated, they can create imbalances in our mental and emotional states.

Keeping the energy flowing smoothly throughout our system promotes a healthier mind and body. It would be wonderful to believe in a utopia where we all lead stress-free lives, but sadly, we live in a fast-paced world where many of us *are* affected by stress. I can't emphasize enough the importance of relieving tension and anxiety on a regular basis, whether it's through massage therapy, yoga, meditation, or physical exercise. Find out what works best for you.

The human body is sustained by the same prana that nourishes the Universe. The body (your equipment) has the ability to control and utilize this special energy by means of *pranayama*. Please don't let the word scare you; it simply means "to *control, channel,* and *direct* the flow of prana through the use of the breath." Prana exists in all things, yet it's completely independent of them.

While we don't go around saying, "I'm running low on prana!" when our body is depleted of it, we often complain of feeling tired or unwell. This is when the breath *must* come first, so when you start wondering, *Why am I looking exhausted, feeling stressed, or just generally out of balance?* stop for a moment and ask yourself where your energy is going and how you've been breathing recently. Consider the way you breathe to be a reflection of how you live your life. If you're using shallow, restricted, or short breaths, it's more than likely that you're holding on to or suppressing your emotions. You're limiting the potential of your life and the true nature of who you really are — and more important, who you can be.

Prana is an essential psychic force, so we should all be aware of its existence. You *can* and *do* have access to this universal reservoir. No one is excluded . . . it's there for everyone. Besides breathing consciously, which helps you physically by bringing more prana into your body, I want to show you how it can help you on a spiritual level. Prana nourishes matter and is the resource that exists in the magnetic field that surrounds all living things (aura) and raises the vibrations of your energy centers (chakras).

Let me guide you through two powerful exercises. The first one is meant to go with the "Mindfulness of Breathing" technique from Chapter 1, using the count of numbers while inhaling, holding, and exhaling each breath. Getting into the rhythm of the breath is more important than striving for its duration.

If you experience dizziness or feel light-headed, stop and take a break until your system adjusts to breathing in this manner. Please take your time and focus on doing the exercises correctly so that you achieve the full benefit.

EXERCISE: Moving the Prana

Find a comfortable place to lie down. This can be either a bed or an exercise mat on the floor. Rest your hands lightly over your *solar plexus* (located right under your ribs, just above your abdomen). Breathe rhythmically. Inhale slowly to the count of four. Hold for two counts, and exhale to the count of four. After another two counts, breathe in again for four counts, hold for two counts, and breathe out to the count of four. Continue for five minutes until you've settled into a steady rhythm throughout the exercise.

After you've established a comfortable rhythm, I want you to use your imagination and willpower to visualize that each *incoming* breath is infused with prana. Remember that you can command this force (just as the yogis do) to flow wherever you wish. Some people find it helpful to visualize prana in the form of sparkling white light. With each breath, try to create a mental picture of the prana streaming in through your nostrils and flowing right down into your lungs. Imagine that this energy is being absorbed and stored in your solar plexus. With each breath, let the energy circulate in your solar-plexus area, as it strengthens your total body and mind.

As you *exhale,* hold on to your will and imagination. Visualize this energy being distributed throughout your body. Feel it soak into every bone, muscle, and nerve ending, from the top of your head to the very tips of your fingers and toes.

This exercise is wonderful if you're feeling tired or need to revitalize yourself. You may experience a tingling sensation on your scalp, forehead, face, or even in your hands and fingers. This is quite normal, and it's a positive sign that you're feeling the effects of the prana and doing the exercise correctly. You also may sense the energy moving back and forth while it cleanses and revitalizes your aura and chakra system. At the same time, it's raising your vibration and replenishing your vital supply of spiritual energy. Once again, don't force this exercise. It should be carried out in a calm and gentle frame of mind as you learn to work with the healing power of the breath.

EXERCISE: Absent Healing

When you become proficient at recharging yourself, you'll be able to share this gift of healing with family and friends who are feeling lethargic or who need some rejuvenating energy — this is known as *absent healing* or *distant healing.* This form of spiritual healing doesn't require recipients to be physically present, as it's possible to transmit healing energy over any distance. Energy doesn't follow the laws of time and space, so it doesn't matter where they are in the world. They may not even be consciously aware that healing has been performed for them, but hopefully they will *feel* the benefits. It's the love and concern that you have for them that matters.

Let's begin the process of sending absent healing. You can either sit or lie down when transmitting energy. Close your eyes, and begin by raising your hands up with your palms facing outward. As you center yourself, focus your awareness on your heart area as you begin to breathe easily and calmly. Imagine a sparkling white light flowing from your palms and your heart center. Say a small prayer to God, the Divine Source, that your soul act as a channel for the healing energy (prana) to flow through you to the person of your choice.

When you begin to see or feel the energy flowing, say the recipient's name out loud or in your mind; and picture him or her well, balanced, and whole. As you focus on this image, notice how healthy the individual looks in his or her eyes, and see that sparkle of light and health beaming there. This healing energy is charged with your love and compassion, so *really* feel those emotions filling you as you send this force to your friend. You can also transmit it to several people, one at a time or even as a group. By sending them this wonderful gift of healing, energy will flow to them and begin to work through the energy field (aura) around them, which in turn will be absorbed by their physical body.

This exercise only takes a few minutes. When you're finished, give thanks to the Source by saying a small prayer. Try washing your hands afterward to cut the connection, or simply shake your fingers toward the ground, where the energy will be absorbed back into the earth. This healing is coming from your heart with love, and to link from the heart means to have a connection, but with a loving detachment so that it's not a drain on your own power.

Absent healing can also be sent to people and places you're not familiar with. If there's trouble in another country due to a disaster, you can send those who live there energy to help their suffering. Imagine the millions of people who looked on in shock after the 9/11 tragedy. The tens of thousands of people who suffered felt and witnessed the love and healing energy coming from all over the world as they tried to come to terms with their losses and rebuild their lives.

If you hear an ambulance in the distance, send its occupants energy. If you learn of a family in need, send them energy. If you find out that a neighbor is about to leave this earth, send him or her energy to make it a peaceful passing. There doesn't have to be an illness in order for you to send healing — you can even send it to a difficult situation. If a friend of yours is separating from a spouse or there's a bad work environment somewhere, these people can benefit from a little healing thought or intention, too. There are no limits once you develop a healing consciousness. As I've said many times, we're all connected. You *can* make a difference.

Your Personal Healing Sanctuary

The power of your imagination is unlimited. Visualization techniques can transport you wherever you want . . . there are no boundaries. When you lead a packed life — running at full tilt, with no time to stop or even to catch your breath — it can be difficult to find a quiet moment for yourself. Yet we all need these times, as they're essential to our overall well-being.

I learned this lesson very early on during my training as a medium. I was taught a visualization technique that I practice whenever I feel myself in need of some healing and relaxation, or when I just need to reflect and simply *be*. This is a time for my soul to be soothed, infused, and recharged with healing energy. When you don't have the opportunity to physically get away, you can go to your own special *healing sanctuary,* and the best part is that it's right there, wherever you are! I was taught how to delve into my own imagination, to visualize and construct a healing sanctuary in my own mind — a tranquil place that's always there, one that I can call my own because I created it.

I want to share the details of my healing sanctuary with you. I made a conscious decision that I wanted somewhere that I could step into — such as a room, as opposed to an open space — so I designed this beautiful room in my mind, as though I were piecing together a jigsaw. It was all my choice. My favorite color is blue, so I chose pale blue walls that shimmer in particular lights. I decorated the room with fresh flowers, plants, and crystals of all different sizes. The crystals actually bounce the light around the room in rainbow colors that dance on the walls as I move about, which has an incredible relaxing effect. In the middle of my room, I placed an amazing table made of polished metal, which is molded to the exact shape of my own body. It's beautifully smooth to the touch, and although it's metal, it's never cold. It's so comfortable to lie on when I want to relax and heal myself.

As I continued to design my room, I constructed a floor-to-ceiling open window in front of the table. As I rest on the molded surface, I have a view of green forests capped with white-topped mountains. The sky is a wonderful turquoise blue. For me, this is utopia, where everything is in perfect harmony. The cool breeze fills the room with scents of the forest.

My sanctuary was almost complete. I imagined small speakers on the walls to play calming music, and I often imagine that I'm bathed in different-colored lights as I lie on the table. The music and light have their own healing qualities. There was one final part of my sanctuary that I decided to add: a small computer with a glowing white neon border so that I can type the questions that I want answered. Every so often, I'll ask one of my guides to join me, or I might call on a healer for a specific problem. My sanctuary was then complete. It fulfills all my healing needs . . . it's my private place when I want to renew my spiritual and emotional strength.

As I've explained earlier, the mind and body do *not* discriminate between sensory images created in your mind and those in reality. The stronger the image you create, the stronger the result will be. Once you design your own healing sanctuary, it will remain with you for the rest of your life whenever you need it. There are times when I visit my sanctuary every week, or I can go months between visits, but when I do step through those doors, the healing energy is intact and just the way I left it. I have all the tools in my imagination, and if I need anything else, I simply visualize it. Now that I've shared my private healing sanctuary, it's time to create yours, a place you can honor and call your very own. . . . Are you ready?

Make sure that you're comfortable, in a place where you're not going to be disturbed for a little while. Once you're settled, use the power of your mind and imagine your *own* special sanctuary. What kind of place would you like it to be? Do you want it to be indoors or outdoors? Is it your favorite beach, or is it a hut on a tropical island surrounded by crystal blue water? Alternatively, you may imagine your sanctuary in a forest or on top of a mountain. Do you want a special password that grants you access to your safe, comfortable haven?

If you choose indoors, is it in a cozy room or a lofty open space? Remember that you can create anything you want. If you want to leave out a ceiling so that you'll be able to see the sun, or the stars at night, that's fine. Imagine the room in your favorite color. Are there pictures, words, mirrors, or decorations hanging on the walls? Select the furniture that you want to place around the room. Let your imagination go as you continue to build your sanctuary, just the way you want it. Make it as real as possible. This is a place to heal your body, mind, and soul, so choose everything to support the process — it's up to you to decide if you want to add or remove anything. Make it a safe, comfortable haven.

Once you've built your sanctuary, it's time to step in and enter your special place for the first time. Look around you and use *all* your senses. Reach out and touch the furniture, walls, decorations, and ornaments. Smell the air and the fragrances of Mother Nature. Listen to the sounds that are close by, as well as those coming from a distance. Feel the warmth of the sun or the coolness of a breeze touch your skin, along with the earth or floor under your feet. Let the wonder of your senses fill your soul.

Make yourself comfortable there, whether you're sitting or lying down. Take a good look around: up, down, and from one side to the other. Is there anything that you'd like to add or change? Visualize it and complete your space. Do you want to give your sanctuary its own personal name? Would you like to bring in a guide or a healer to assist you with any question or problem that you hope to address? Do you want to invite anyone else in, perhaps someone you love or someone you may have an issue with, to create a more positive outcome in your physical world? Anything is possible!

No matter what type of healing sanctuary you create, it will always be there for you. Just close your eyes and imagine yourself stepping into it again. Go there as often as you want. The more you visit, the stronger the image will become. Remember that this is your healing sanctuary, a wondrous place for you and your soul to retreat to when you need a little respite from the pressures of the outside world.

CHAPTER SIX

Breaking Free:
Turning the Past
into a Bridge
for the Future

W e've covered much of the groundwork for understanding the awesome power of the soul. Now it's time for you go on to the next level of your awareness and growth. You could be doing all this work in order to become more enlightened, and that's great. However, to really end your pain, suffering, and discontent and achieve more peace and happiness in your life — that is, to become even more attuned to your soul — it's important that you deal with the ultimate human challenge between the ego-self and the soul.

When negative feelings and thoughts are instilled in your ego-self, they create disharmony, emotional instability, worry, and negative behavioral patterns. When you make time to explore and heal your different viewpoints and belief systems, you'll have a stronger stand against the insecurities stemming from your ego-self, giving your soul the opportunity to move forward and soar to new heights. You'll experience a deeper awareness of yourself and others, and by doing so, you'll choose a path that will be more in sync with your inner vision.

I know so many people who display natural raw talents and could be so successful if only they'd see what others see in them. This strikes a chord with me, too, as I recall my own background when I was starting to practice as a medium. I was riddled with self-doubts, such as: *Will I be good enough? Will the evidence I present be validated? What will people think of me?* My constant battle with the fear coming from my own mind eventually lessened as colleagues and friends who saw the talent I possessed kept reminding me that I had something unique, something that I was passionate about: a gift that could help and heal others. Somehow I had to learn to let go of the doubts that would hold me back and take a fresh approach to my thinking process. A metaphor that I really like is viewing life as a merry-go-round: Sometimes it's safer to stay on than jump off. It's the fear of the unknown — or worse still, it's the problem of how to get back on after falling off.

My doubts stemmed from my upbringing, since I'd never received praise for anything I did well or encouragement to strive and be whatever I wanted to be. My sights had been set low for me. I constantly worried if I'd be able do this work well and whether I could handle the responsibility of being a lifeline for so many people whose souls were hurting and who were suffering through personal bereavement.

Worry is an extension of fear and can be a shattering blow to your personal and spiritual development. Generally, you worry more about things that you consciously think about, rather than physical dangers such as a flood or a hurricane. It's all about how you were conditioned. I want to encourage you to start breaking free from past habits, restrictions, and behavioral traits. Let go of that mind-set of worry. Cast aside those limitations that have held you back. Stop using language such as: "If only I had . . ." or "If only I had been . . ." You possess one soul and one life in this body — why live a *could've, would've,* or *should've* existence? As you expand your mind and explore new belief systems, you'll embark on a path of endless opportunities that serve you, your needs, and your soul for your highest good.

Breaking Free of Worry

Do you sometimes feel that you were born to worry? Can you think of someone right now who deserves the title of "The Chronic Worrier"? People often tell me what they're agonizing over — but then again, they always have. Even as a child, people poured out their cares and problems to me, regardless of whether they knew me or not. Nowadays, I know that comes with the territory of what I do for a living. I have a deep empathy for people who worry, as I know what it's like, having been a perpetual worrier myself. I was raised in an alcoholic home, so anxiety has become second nature to me.

People often say to me: "John, how can you worry? Aren't you a psychic?" Even though I'm blessed with this wonderful gift, I'm still very much a human being. Some people think that stewing over things will somehow protect them or prepare them for the unexpected. I'm sorry to dispel this myth, but it doesn't work that way. When you worry, it interrupts your natural rhythm, affecting all areas of your life and eating away at your time — time that could be used for enjoying life, as well as for reflection, relaxing and quieting your mind, meditating, and being with yourself and your soul. When you worry, you're demonstrating a lack of trust in God, the Divine Source. You came from the Source and are one with It, so know and trust that It's working to help you all the time.

I remember some years ago when I did a screen test for a TV pilot about psychics and mediums. I was one of three chosen to audition to be the host for the show. In the television business, everything becomes frenetic once the idea is launched, but that initial spurt of activity is usually followed by a long period of waiting. So I waited and waited some more. I felt that the show was a good fit and I wanted to be part of it. Of course I started worrying whether I was going to get the deal. After even more waiting, I eventually received a call to say that I hadn't been selected. I felt disappointed, and the mental chatter started up with a vengeance: *Why wasn't I picked? Wasn't I good enough? I really could have used this opportunity. So now what?*

This would have been a good time for me to remember that it's important not to let anxiety take over your entire thinking process. Worry breeds worry. After I received the bad news, a wise friend called me and said, "Why are you feeling so down? You know you didn't get this because it wasn't meant to be, and something else will come along that'll be better!" Sure enough, some time later I did get a call for another television project that was an even better fit for my personality and my abilities — and I got the job! If there's a moral to this story, it's probably this: The original show that I auditioned for never made it on the air! I learned an interesting lesson, which has become one of my personal mantras: *All I can do is my best, so let go of the outcome.* When you adopt this attitude, it's more fun and less worry!

This chapter is all about breaking free, and I wanted to include a section specifically dedicated to worry's crippling effect on the soul. So many of us let this emotion take over our lives. It holds us back in its tight grip, never letting us move forward in a positive direction. It can literally close down our creative abilities and prevent us from achieving our full potential and expanding our soul's capacity. It can stop us in our tracks, holding us there temporarily, or in some cases, on a more permanent basis.

If you're going to lead an expansive and soul-fulfilled life, then part of the process of breaking free is to learn to stop worrying. Of course, there are going to be times when it's legitimate to feel concern. It's impossible not to worry if a relative is seriously ill or a friend is going through a personal crisis. However, I'm talking about when worry gets in the way of living; causes you stress; and stops you from sleeping, relaxing, and enjoying life to the fullest — when it starts to suffocate your soul.

Many of us aren't even aware when we're worrying. That's the nature of habit-forming characteristics. Becoming aware is an important part of anxiety reduction. As you become more conscious of the habit of worrying, it's possible to develop the ability to switch it off before it takes over. Worry can be set off by something as simple as watching the news on television with all the graphic images. If you're the sort of person who's affected by the news, it's possible that it will push you into a state of anxiety and stress. You can't change the world, but you *can* change yourself.

By working on ourselves, we're nourishing the overall positive consciousness of the world that we're all connected to. Now let's take a few minutes to identify what we worry about most. Here are just a few examples of some typical concerns:

- Our families
- Our finances
- Our careers (or lack thereof)
- What other people think of us
- Whether we're too fat or too thin
- Going to the doctor or dentist
- Rising fuel costs
- Exams and tests
- Other people's problems

Often we worry because it's all that we know how to do — and for some of us, we even worry about how much we're worrying! Anxiety is a mental state that can restrict our growth. It's easy to identify those of us who have this problem; it's written all over our faces. Our brows are furrowed with worry lines. Frequently, our health is also affected.

I know an amazing gentleman, Derek, whom I met many years ago. He has so much talent, is well educated, and deserves a great career as a public speaker, yet he worries about the very thing he was trained for. I've seen him, and he's a dynamic speaker, but his worries hold him back. He undervalues himself and sells himself short. You can almost hear his mind working and fretting as he asks himself: *Will I be interesting? Will the audience like me? Am I wearing the right clothes? Do I have a stage presence? What happens if everyone walks out halfway through?* One simple worry becomes ten . . . and then even more. It's like a cancer cell — it just keeps multiplying. The doubts become so big that he starts to believe them, but they *can* be cured.

In the case of Derek, he worked with a life coach who encouraged him, telling him that it was time to break the cycle of those disempowering mental habits — in other words, it was time to stop living with all the self-doubts of the past and embrace the moment and the amazing opportunities waiting in the future.

People who worry usually remember their failures rather than their successes. When Derek altered his consciousness, he truly began to change his life. If you relate to Derek's story, it's now time to break free and start building *your* bridge for the future. In the following sections, I'll give you some techniques to help you beat this form of mental torment. Every time you deal with and overcome an aspect of worry, your confidence builds, and you begin to do what you want in life with enthusiasm and passion.

Keeping Busy = Worrying Less

There are many ways of preventing worry from crippling and suffocating your life. One of them is to keep busy. When your schedule is full, you really don't have time to worry. People with too much time on their hands will often spend it feeling anxious. So if you're a born worrier, try to recognize those occasions when you catch yourself worrying the most. Journal your thoughts for a few weeks, identifying the times or places in which you find yourself feeling apprehensive, and see what triggers this feeling. Keep track of how often worry occurs. I carry around a pocket recorder, which is a great little device. I use it to record notes to myself that I often transcribe later — it's better than carrying around a notepad. Remember that you're not avoiding issues; rather, you're trying to change your mental programming.

You have to find alternative things to do during those critical worry times. Shake things up and change your routine around. For example, if you find that one of the key times you worry is after work when you go home, use that period to start a new project — something that will occupy and challenge your mind. Is there an evening class or workshop that you've always wanted to take, one that would enhance your job or maybe just get you doing something completely different? Be your own spiritual coach and support yourself with positive affirmations; eat a healthy, balanced diet; and exercise on your own or join a gym. It's also important to get out of the house and connect with nature as often as you can.

Being productive can lead to increased happiness, as you achieve more and worry less. Imagine how you're going to feel when you're using your time more effectively, not worrying as much, relaxing more, and at the same time advancing your career and surpassing what you thought possible. The whole process has a ripple effect as your family, friends, and co-workers see and feel the change in you and start emulating your positive actions and integrating them into *their* lives. Everybody wins!

Being Perfect Isn't Always the Answer

Another way of preventing worry is to stop being such a perfectionist. You don't have to do everything flawlessly. It's mainly in the mind that you worry about doing everything just right. I've learned to replace *perfectionism* with *permission* to be human. I've always had artistic talent, and when I take drawing classes, I don't set out to create a masterpiece — I just draw to the best of my ability. I'm happy being in the present and just simply enjoy the time drawing.

When you adopt this attitude, you'll worry less and be happier in the process. I know someone who's meticulous about everything he does. We tease him endlessly and call him "Mr. Bullet Point" because every time he sends an e-mail or creates a document, it's guaranteed to have some bullet points in it! He can't finish it unless it's beautifully formatted and everything is consistent, but here's the serious part — he applies this to every aspect of his life. He worries if he hasn't analyzed every outcome, considered all angles, checked, and double-checked. He's unable to conquer his compulsion to be perfect. It's his mental approach that forces him to work this way. Since worrying is an extension of fear, and his biggest fear is not being in control, perfectionism is just another way of staying in control.

It can be a dangerous situation to get into: You worry so much about your reputation that, in the end, it suffers to such an extent that you have no reputation left to speak of. There's a middle ground here, one that encompasses "peace of mind." Also, if you're someone who constantly postpones everything, it can be symptomatic of this form of "perfectionistic" worry. You may have found yourself saying that you can't invite people over for dinner until the dining room is redecorated, or that you shouldn't apply for that new job until you've gained more experience — or the myriad other excuses to put something off until tomorrow.

Postponing is just another form of worry. It's about wanting to make sure that things are perfect before moving ahead. There are legitimate occasions when you're going to want to do something perfectly, but there are just as many times when the old saying "Actions speak louder than words" must prevail. Sometimes you just have to get on and do it rather than dither. So don't always wait for conditions to be ideal — they may never be. Do *something!* It's better than doing *nothing*. Give yourself a break! Yes, relax, ease up, and don't attempt to be perfect all the time. Try being happy instead!

EXERCISE: Rearranging Your Mental Landscape

It's impossible to come up with blanket advice that suits everyone. People are affected by worry in different ways, and there's no one method to completely heal or cure it, regardless of the circumstances. Some people may even need therapy or counseling, but it's healthy to take a look at your life from time to time and try some basic cognitive restructuring. There are a few simple steps that you can take. The following exercise is a good way of helping manage your habits of worry.

1. Make a list of what you dwell on the most. Identify what you think about when you worry. Try to listen to your internal dialogue. Keep a note of these thoughts. Allow yourself only so much time to worry, then move on.

2. Once you've gotten into the routine of journaling your worry thoughts, take your notes and spend some time analyzing each thought. What's the evidence for it? Is it likely to happen? Has it ever happened before? Finally, is there any logical reason to believe that it ever *will* happen? If not, cross it off the list with a big red pen!

3. What's the worst thing that could occur? Plan out how you'd handle it. What actions could you take to minimize the effect? Write down what you *need* to do.

4. As you keep your journal of these worries and the possible actions you might take, try to write them down in two columns so that the new thoughts form a positive outcome.

5. When you worry, you tend to imagine the worst thing that could happen, but you can also imagine the *best* thing that could happen. Try turning it around!

6. Meditate and practice the "Relaxing the Body" exercise, and begin to talk to your higher self and ask if there's another way you can let go of a particular worry or concern. Be open and ask if there's some other advice that you need to hear at this time.

As you start making subtle changes in the way you think, how much you worry, or what you worry about, remember this: Any adjustments that you attempt to make will only be temporary unless you own them yourself. No one else can make them happen for you . . . only you! You have to be responsible for your own transformation. Believing that you *should* change isn't enough; you have to tell yourself that you *must* change — that you *can* change.

Breaking Free of Psychological Fears

There are a number of factors that can prevent you from achieving your soul's purpose of being all that you can be. Sometimes the root causes that hold you back are undetectable. For example, you may feel as though you're being held a prisoner, especially if you're living with psychological fears that have been instilled in you, whether by others or yourself. This conditioning could be caused by some major event in the past or by something that's happening right now. When mental programming becomes negative, you have a tendency to exist in a fear-based world, which in turn creates fear-based thoughts such as:

- *What do other people think of me?*
- *I'm going to fail.*
- *It's too late for me.*
- *I'll make the same mistake again.*

Each one of these can become a major limiting factor in your daily life, if you choose to let it. These mental patterns get lodged in your subconscious and can affect your future thoughts. Your behavior then follows what's been programmed into your mind and psyche.

These programs have the power to become quite destructive and will rob your soul, as well as your life, of precious energy. Such psychological handcuffs will take away the opportunity to express your full potential, unless you learn to break free of them.

I want to help you explore these limiting fear-based thoughts and find some ways to deal with them so that you can eradicate them from your mind and life. Beneath these thoughts, you have the ability and power as a soul to be a healthy, positive force in your own life, bringing in more energy, happiness, wisdom, and healing.

It would be easy to write a whole book on this sensitive subject, but I want to assist you in breaking free of some of the more common limiting thoughts that affect us all. Once again (and it probably won't be for the last time), I want to remind you that you're a soul connected to the Divine Source. Trust and know that you're meant to be happy and whole, not held prisoner by the psychological conditioning of your past or your ego-self. To change, ultimately you must *recognize* and become *aware* of the negative behavior patterns in your life so that you can process and correct them, now and in the future, as they emerge. In doing so, you'll increase the opportunity to be in total harmony with your life, your soul, and yourself.

The "What Others Think of Me" Syndrome

How many times have you been at a party and you didn't say anything during a group discussion for fear of what the other people might think of you, or out of the belief that you had nothing important to add? Do you worry that you're not educated enough to fit in some social circles? Equally, you're probably concerned about what people will think if you wear a certain outfit, one that perhaps stands out in a crowd. This form of negative thinking creates worry about how others perceive you, and it stifles your creativity and personal expression. It can prevent you from having *fun* or even going to the places you like most.

We've *all* been guilty of this at some point or another, and I really believe that we spend far more time worrying about what others may think of us than we should. Just remember that they're probably just as worried about what we think of them! People are far too involved in their own lives to devote a lot of time to what's going on in ours.

Have you noticed that at certain times when you're about to take on a new project or endeavor, there's always someone there to put you down, laugh, or tell you that you'll never accomplish it? Why think negatively about it yourself when there are plenty of people to do it for you? When you exert energy trying to live up to the expectations of others (I'm not talking about your responsibilities to your family, close friends, or work) and you don't meet them, you become their slave. Don't be too concerned about what others think — after all, it's *your* life, and you should only be concerned about what and how *you* think, or how well you treat yourself. People will always have an opinion, but it's theirs, not yours. The only person who really knows you is *you*.

Steps for Breaking Free of the "What Others Think of Me" Syndrome

1. Have trust and faith in yourself — it's your opinion that matters.

2. Meditate and visualize a healthy image of yourself.

3. Work on your self-esteem and confidence. The more you do so, the more self-confident and powerful you'll become.

4. Surround yourself with friends who aren't always talk-
    ing about everyone else. Remember that they will often
    have just as many hang-ups as you, or in some cases,
    even more!

5. Don't let others set the pace. It's your life — live it and
    let others live theirs.

6. If you're attending a function and meeting new people,
    say the affirmation: "Wherever I go, there are friends
    there." This statement really relieves a lot of stress or
    tension in such a situation. Acknowledge that there are
    plenty of people who will accept you just as you are.

7. Pay someone a compliment and make that person feel
    good — in turn, maybe that individual will turn around
    and do the same in his or her life.

The "I'm Going to Fail" Syndrome

This is another common form of disempowering, negative
thinking. How many times have you gone to an interview, saying
to yourself, "I haven't got a chance in hell of getting this job!"? As
a teenager, do you recall expecting to fail your driving test before
you'd even taken it? We've already discussed the law of attraction:
"Life follows thought." Are you creating a negative outcome as
a result of your fear and past conditioning? It all comes down to
how much you truly believe in yourself and your self-worth. It's
important to see yourself as a winner.

Leela was a student of mine in Los Angeles some years ago. During one of my workshops, she told her fellow classmates how her
fear of failure was crippling her life. She'd volunteered her time for
the past four years at a local cable station to educate herself enough
to eventually become a TV director. She loved being there, working
with the cameras and the production staff, helping build and break
down the sets, and learning all she could about directing. When

she talked about her job at the station, you could hear the passion in her words, and her soul would just light up. She devoted much of her free time to the station but had no regrets. She was happy doing what she loved and being around creative people.

It was at the end of the fourth year when Leela started to feel that she was ready to take on a job as an assistant producer. There was a position advertised at a local television studio, so she applied for the job and submitted her show reel featuring some of the projects she'd worked on.

A few days later, she received a call from the studio saying how impressed they were with her work and inviting her in for an interview. She was offered the job. Leela was very excited and prepared to start work the very next week. Her elation was short-lived, though, as her mind and ego-self started talking her out of it. She wasn't listening to reason or her intuition, and her ego was getting the better of her. It was as if her mind were running wild, chattering and jumping from thought to thought, spinning out of control and leaving her feeling dazed and confused. She started to convince herself that she'd never be able to do the job or live up to her employer's expectations. She was consumed with the fear of failing.

Unfortunately, people who settle for less usually get it. Leela's negative conditioning got the best of her, and she took an office job instead, working 9 to 5 in a cubicle. I heard from her recently, and she's slowly making her way back to her more creative soul-self by working on her past negative programming and identifying where the conditioning occurred in her life. She's been reprogramming her mind with positive thoughts and visualizations, and she told me that she's about to apply for another television job. She admitted that from time to time the negative thoughts still surface, but now she's developed the skills to prevent them from taking her prisoner.

Steps for Breaking Free of the "I'm Going to Fail" Syndrome

1. Work on letting go of past beliefs, fears, and hang-ups. Begin having positive conversations with yourself.

2. Start believing why you can, as opposed to why you can't.

3. Stay focused on your goals and aspirations.

4. Write all your experiences in your journal. Get them out of your head!

5. Think of yourself as a winner rather than a loser. Once you believe in yourself, you'll be surprised by how much more other people start believing in you. Remember this statement: "We train others how to treat us by the way we treat ourselves."

6. Believe in success. When you begin thinking that you can succeed, you'll find that your mind starts to figure out solutions for success. You won't even contemplate failure.

7. Visualize and feel yourself achieving a positive outcome and living a life that you know you'll love.

8. Know that all you can really do is give every opportunity your best shot!

The "It's Too Late for Me" Syndrome

We all know people who've reached a certain age and are stuck in the mind-set that they'll remain single for the rest of their lives. All too often, you hear them say: "I'm too old — I'm not going to meet anyone now." The same goes for those who feel that a promotion has passed them by and now it's too late. This is just another form of being held hostage by your psychological fear. It's *never* too late. I love the quote by George Eliot: "It is never too late to be what you might have been."

A client recently told me a story about her aunt, who at the age of 70 went back to college to get a degree in English. Was it too late for her? She clearly didn't think so. I just watched a television show featuring a happy, lively 82-year-old man windsurfing on the ocean alongside all the 20-something surfer dudes. Apparently, he didn't believe he was too old for anything! When you make such excuses, you block positive people and situations from manifesting themselves in your life — people and situations that could bring you unlimited amounts of spirit energy, passion, and joy. The soul is ageless and eternal, which is why so many people say, "I really don't feel *that* old."

In reality, it's your physical body that ages, not your soul. By tapping into your soul and the power of spirit that flows through it, you can feel youthful, since spirit brings energy and vitality to your physical body when you need it. It all comes down to how you approach life and how you're taking care of yourself. If you really believe that you're too old, then you know what happens: You just get older.

I've known many people who don't give in to the whole notion of what one can or can't do at a particular age. It's societal conditioning that dictates how we should act at a certain age. As I mentioned before, my assistant, Gretchen, has a very young-minded mother in her mid-80s who has a boyfriend, still drives her car, and volunteers once a week at a homeless shelter. I've seen people in their 30s act older than my assistant's mom. I hope that I'm that young at heart when I'm in my 80s!

Steps for Breaking Free of the "It's Too Late for Me" Syndrome

1. Adopt an attitude of "It's never too late."

2. Try something new every day. You're never too old to try.

3. Believe in yourself.

4. Don't listen to others if they say you're too old. If you're passionate about something, you can achieve it!

5. Associate with people who *do* rather than *say.*

6. Enroll in an evening class that you've always wanted to join.

7. Refuse to let your excuses hinder your potential experiences.

8. Don't live a life of regrets.

The "I'll Make the Same Mistake Again" Syndrome

If everyone adopted this attitude, we'd be in a sorry state. For example, most successful inventions have resulted from years of experiments and mistakes. Thankfully, most inventors haven't subscribed to this philosophy. As a child, when you fell off your bike, what did you parents say? "Get back on!"

If you want to be successful, then adopt a healthy attitude toward mistakes. It's important to make them if we're to grow and learn. I love what the late actress Tallulah Bankhead once said: "If I had to live my life again, I'd make the same mistakes, only sooner." Being wrong is a wonderful way of seeing what doesn't work, and it offers you greater insight into how to achieve what you do want. I have no problem making mistakes, as I know that they're my greatest teachers. When I commit an error, it's a chance for me to stop, listen, and ask myself: *What am I supposed to be learning here, and how can I make the situation better?* I suggest that you do the same. Your blunders are great transformative tools, in that they provide you with opportunities to learn about your weaknesses, what should be changed, and any areas that may need improvement. I make it my intention to see mistakes as blessings in disguise.

I remember one time I made the error in judgment of *not* listening to my intuition. I was about to drive 200 miles to give a demonstration, and the organizers were expecting a large audience. Several days before, I kept getting a nagging feeling that I should call them and make sure that everything was okay and check that they had all the sound equipment for the evening. Instead, my rational mind kicked in and said, "No, John. They're professionals; they've done this hundreds of times before — let it go."

Of course, this was one of those occasions when I should have *really* listened to my intuition. I arrived to find out that they had a broken microphone system, a child's stool (only 12 inches high) for me to perch on, and no air conditioning on that muggy New England night when the temperature was still 89 degrees. In addition, the spotlight was so powerful that it could have lit up New York City! I should have honored and trusted my feelings and followed through with the decision to call the organizers. By doing so, I could have saved a lot of aggravation for myself as well as for the poor staff who rushed around trying to fix everything. I vowed to myself that I wouldn't make *that* mistake again.

Steps for Breaking Free of the "I'll Make the Same Mistake Again" Syndrome

1. You're human, so give yourself permission to err from time to time.

2. Learn from the mistake so that you don't make it again. Turn down the volume of your ego-self's mind chatter. Learn to accept being wrong without beating yourself up.

3. Take any feedback rather than getting angry — it's a great resource for learning.

4. Listen to your intuition. If it's guiding you in the right way, then have faith and trust in yourself.

5. Learn from other people's blunders and incorporate them into your life.

6. Laugh at some of your mistakes . . . it's better than beating yourself up.

7. Journal your errors, what you learned from them, and what steps you took; that way, you can always go back and see them in a positive light.

Cutting Ties with the Past

If you want to give yourself the best chance of success, then you're going to have to cut some of your ties with the past. I'm referring to those ties — in other words, the limiting factors — that constantly hold you back. They could be causing blockages preventing your soul from experiencing and learning.

As the soul learns from our experiences, we end up taking these lessons through our lives, but many of us are held back by legacies of the past. When the past retains such a strong hold on the present, it can often be enough to derail the strongest of us. Legacies can be anything from issues related to one's upbringing in a troubled family or being bullied at school to an accident that we may never have gotten over or even a failed relationship . . . the list of possible legacies is endless. Until we make the conscious decision to cut ties with whichever one we're dealing with, it will continue to influence our life. If it involves emotions of guilt or shame, then it becomes even more important to sever it, as the guilt complex causes us embarrassment, inhibits our actions, destroys self-confidence, and sparks worry.

Let's examine some techniques for how to cut ties with the past so that you can start to create a bridge for the future. I want to use the case study of a young woman I know named Sarah. She had unlimited potential, yet she was hampered by many legacies from the past. Some of these were real, physical ties related to family issues of dysfunctionality. Sarah was sent to a strict school that instigated a deep and long-lasting legacy of worthlessness, so feelings of inadequacy were implanted in her at an impressionable young age. No matter how many original, creative, or worthwhile ideas she had, her teachers were quick to chide her and shoot them down in flames. She carried this mental baggage into adulthood, and it manifested into a series of major hurdles that prevented her from reaching her full potential.

Decades later, she still brought up these negative, soul-robbing memories from her past. She was prone to helping other people all the time as a way of avoiding the problem of dealing with her own issues. I often reminded her that she'd be quite phenomenal if she could only get out of her own way. She'd taken endless self-help workshops, yet she was still stuck and just couldn't seem to get her life together. It was akin to a form of soul leakage or fragmentation. She needed to stop selling herself short — it was as though her subconscious or ego-self had an almost toxic contempt for her potential, acting like a nasty voice inside her head, constantly criticizing and discouraging her. She was eager to please, partly out of concern over what people might think of her, and partly due to her need for constant praise.

She became a caretaker for her elderly parents, devoting considerable time every week to driving a 140-mile round-trip to ferry them to doctors' appointments, take them shopping, cook them meals, and deal with all their financial matters. I do want to point out here that there's nothing wrong with helping your folks as they get older. Most of us do it, and it's admirable as long as it's balanced with everything else and doesn't overwhelm your life.

In Sarah's case, it was time to sever some of her ties with the past so that the *energy cords* (which I talked about earlier) could start the essential healing process, letting the energy flow back into her system. Her biggest challenge would be the personal migration from helping others and being "Miss Fix-It" to helping herself. This required some precognitive behavior, noticing and seeing the signs when her Miss Fix-It personality was about to emerge.

But for Sarah, there were other more physical issues that she had to deal with, such as her pattern of avoidance.

A typical example of her avoidance tactics was the fact that she had more than five years of tax returns to complete, with boxes and boxes of receipts, bills, and invoices. She literally didn't know where to start. In this case, the hurdle had become so high that for her it was an unscalable wall. She'd gotten adept at finding any excuse not to deal with it. A friend stepped in and introduced Sarah to a new accountant, who devised a process of breaking everything down into more manageable pieces, creating a simple paper-based process that enabled her to tackle the problem on her terms. Instead of listening to her inner critic, who would have normally chided her and goaded her, saying, *You'll never come to grips with this. It's not even worth tackling it, since you won't finish,* she told herself that she could and would sort this mess out once and for all.

As she completed the first year, she was able to hand it over to her accountant; and within eight weeks, all the tax returns were completed and handed over. The boxes that had been stacked up against her wall for years were suddenly gone, and she felt exhilarated! The net result was extraordinary: Not only had one huge hurdle been removed, but far more important, she'd learned how to use the same process in the future. She'd equipped herself with the power to deal with her accounting, rather than avoiding it.

The smile on her face was one of empowerment. All the ties — including the feelings of guilt, embarrassment, and shame — just evaporated overnight. It was a form of emancipation for Sarah. Through the isolated case of her tax returns, she'd found a process that was her bridge, built on a solid foundation of understanding and a renewed sense of her own ability. She now had a formula that worked for her:

1. She'd break up the large obstacles into smaller ones and deal with them on an individual basis.

2. She'd seek out professionals to help her set up a process that she could cope with on her terms.

3. She'd create realistic timescales to lessen the pressure.

Once she removed the mental barrier caused by the constant worry over doing her tax returns, she was able to free herself up to devote some time to her creative pursuits. The success of dealing with her accounting fed her soul. Sarah had learned an important life lesson and had overcome one of her fears — namely, that of not being able to see something through to the end. She consciously cut that tie! She was then ready to sever more of the energy cords that were holding her hostage, one by one. I was really proud of her.

When something becomes so big, sometimes it's easier to push it aside rather than face it head-on. Many of us go through our lives avoiding confrontation and opt for the easier route. In doing so, we're draining our soul's battery bit by bit. By confronting, dealing with, and resolving these hurdles and barriers, we're able to move ahead in a straight line, feeding our soul with the positive energy of renewed self-empowerment.

Throughout this period, Sarah had to learn some painful lessons, including recognizing that there are times when it's important to shield yourself from others to protect your soul. The only way that she was going to move forward was to stop taking on the energy of others by trying to solve their problems. If all energy were positive, that wouldn't be an issue, but the nature of the world we live in is such that people have their own challenges, and some of them will have negative energy.

Sarah is now constantly trying to better herself, affirming that she and her opinion do matter. She's had some positive results through her own actions as well as by talking to others in group therapy, and she's started to surround herself with people who really care about her. Her past has become her bridge, leading her to a healthier and brighter future, and it's up to her to walk across it.

I'm sure that on some level, Sarah's story will resonate with you. It's important to identify what you *feel* is holding you back. Take a critical look and see what's there. When you take time out to do so, you'll be amazed by what you find. This is when the work can truly start. Breathing life into your soul by cutting the ties that prevent the flow of energy is a liberating experience. You'll feel more capable, more alive, more purposeful — more *you!*

Cleaning Out Your Mental Closet

From your early education, the nature of your upbringing, and even the media influences, you're aware when you do something wrong, and it causes embarrassment or even guilt. Embarrassment is usually triggered when you sense that you've acted in a way that your friends, colleagues, or family would disapprove of. This causes feelings of: *I'm not as intelligent as they are,* or *They're better than me,* or *I've made a total ass of myself.* These are all ways that we allow a form of "cancer" to spread. I'm not talking about cancer as it's popularly known — the disease that scientists are working so hard to cure — but rather, I'm referring to a form of psychological cancer that eats away at your very psyche, causing *dis-ease* within your soul.

By subconsciously telling yourself that you're stupid, dumb, or a lesser person, you're letting deposits of this psychological cancer take up residence and spread inside your mental closet. Once it takes hold of your subconscious, it's not something that external radiation treatment or drugs are going to be able to cure. Those things treat biological tissue . . . only *you* can treat psychological tissue with the power of the mind. It's sometimes easier to push things under the rug (which is another way of saying that you're burying the skeletons in your mental closet), but that's not the answer. Eventually, all these issues that have guilt, embarrassment, and other emotions attached to them will become too much to store: They'll literally burst out. You know that at some point you're going to have to deal with them — and no matter what they are, there's usually a good dose of guilt connected with them.

Guilt is highly destructive, as it can eat away at our soul and rob us of our spirit force. It's not limited to the more obvious triggers such as infidelity, deceit, or betrayal, which come about when we've hurt someone. Within the human soul reside many mysteries about our frailties, our fears, and our shame that can be dark and deep. We all know when we're feeling guilty — perhaps we've told a blatant lie or even cheated in some way, whether it was at school or in business.

Guilt feeds directly to the soul. Both guilt and embarrassment have a similar effect: They eat away at your very psyche, destroying your confidence, causing worry, and making you act cautiously; and by doing so, they inhibit your actions. At times, the guilt is so severe that it can cause a type of emotional coma in which the subconscious is in total protection mode, sabotaging all feelings. It doesn't want to face up to or deal with the root cause. That's the point when you literally close down emotionally, and it can be a dark and lonely place. In such situations, I urge caution — it's important to seek professional and/or medical advice.

It's easy to recognize people who are feeling guilty or embarrassed, since it's written all over their face . . . you know, when they can't look you straight in the eye, or they're sweating a little more than usual. It's their body showing the physical signs of what's going on internally, both mentally and emotionally. If left untreated, it's common to experience headaches, back pain, indigestion, and a whole host of other minor ailments.

Yet we all suffer from guilt and embarrassment in our lives at one point or another — some of the time we don't have control over it, and other times we do. For example, if you got fired from your job due to downsizing, as opposed to your poor performance, you're probably going to feel guilty that perhaps you could have done better, but it may in fact have had nothing to do with you at all. During the late '90s, the high-tech sector was a classic case of companies soaring to dizzying heights, only to collapse in a pile of dust sometimes as little as a year or two later. The fallout in terms of human casualties was severe. I heard stories of people being herded like cattle into rooms on a Friday afternoon to be told that they were no longer required. They were issued their papers and told to go home!

You may be a compulsive gambler to the extent that you're squandering money that was put aside to feed the family or for your kid's education. Alternatively, you might be concealing the fact that someone in your family is having trouble with substance abuse. You can't hide these things forever. You have to take responsibility, and by doing so, you start to own the problem. Sometimes it's necessary to bring these things out into the open.

Everyone I know has some skeleton or other. I'm not saying that you have to go around wearing a badge announcing: "I've spent the family's money" or "I got fired!" No, I'm saying that by allowing the feelings of guilt, shame, or embarrassment to prevail, you're only going to exacerbate the mental chaos and allow the deposits of the psychological cancer to spread even further. Remember that you're not alone — there are so many support groups out there to help you. Equally, it can be quite cathartic to have a good "talk session" with a close friend, since just verbalizing things can be the first step in getting help.

There are thousands — often millions — of people who've fallen into the same trap or suffered similar events. You can almost guarantee that when others make a big deal about something that you did and adopt the higher moral ground, they're covering up their own feelings of guilt and shame due to a situation that happened to them in their past. Let it out.

We've all been there in one way or another, so you're never alone. Ultimately, we're all more alike than we dare to realize.

CHAPTER SEVEN

Journey
of the Soul

T here are many mysteries in this world, but one fact is undeniable: Everything is *always* on its way somewhere. If you think about it, even a drop of rain from the clouds eventually ends up back where it came from. Raindrops fall, filling up the lakes, rivers, streams, and tributaries. As the water approaches a waterfall, it rushes forward, gaining energy as it cascades down its relentless path with constant determination toward its ultimate destination. Some of the water is allocated for human use and filtered into our homes for consumption. Some is used to tender the crops that provide us with the food we eat. Eventually, though, all the water goes back into the system for recycling or discharges its energy into the ocean to become part of the collective. Yet, a good proportion evaporates along the way, going back into the sky to fall as rain again . . . and so the cycle starts all over.

Like water, we humans are simply passing through. Everything in this world is perpetually moving, and change is inevitable. As a soul, you're constantly evolving and advancing with grace and humility on your way somewhere, whether you realize it or not. Throughout each lifetime, you'll experience and absorb all its memories and emotions, as well as your own unique personality, into your soul. Just like the raindrop, you'll eventually journey back to where you originated — the spirit world. Only then can you be reborn again and return to this one. Your soul doesn't have an end . . . life is continuous.

Every decision you made in former lives and in the more recent past — and especially those you're making in the present — will be vital to your soul's journey in the future. Your soul knows what it needs to evolve and will continue to steer you in the direction that it wants for its highest good. You may not always follow its prompts, but it will continue to nudge and guide you as you move forward in this life. As you heed its sage guidance, notice how people, situations, and synchronicities start to appear along the way.

The soul is like a powerful magnet continually drawing in the conditions that it needs in order to learn, thrive, and evolve. If someone had told me 20 years ago that I'd be teaching, lecturing, and demonstrating in front of thousands of people, I would have thought that he or she was crazy. Yet as I look back, I can see how my soul steered, prodded, and often pushed me in a direction that led me to this point. Trust that your soul knows what's best as your journey unfolds. Try to meet it halfway by slowing down, listening to, and acknowledging the wisdom from within that's showing up and guiding you in your outside world.

Reincarnation: Here We Go Again

I believe that at one time or another we all experience that incredible moment when we meet someone whom we feel we've known our entire life. No matter how much we try to remember where we encountered this individual previously, the memory just eludes us. Equally, we might be in a different country for the first time yet feel as though we've been there before, as if we've walked the streets and tasted the air. In other words, there's an innate sense of knowing.

I experienced this phenomenon for myself many years ago. I remember how nervous I felt about going to the U.K. to study mediumship. I'd never traveled to Europe, yet as soon as I arrived, I felt totally comfortable — almost *too* comfortable. I asked myself why I felt so at ease from the very first moment I arrived. Why was I so at peace? As I developed new friendships, people would comment on how I seemed to just get along with everyone. Considering that I had a totally different upbringing, I was surprised by how much I took to

British customs, and I acclimated quite well to the lifestyle, as if I'd lived there since birth. I wasn't even fazed by the quirky humor, the strange mannerisms, or the British reticence and reserve. I sampled the meat pies as well as the fish-and-chips, and I even enjoyed the weather, although I'd complain, "It's bone-chillingly cold!" I came to realize that in some past lifetime, I may very well have lived in England, even if it had been hundreds of years earlier.

I've always found the subject of reincarnation intriguing. I think it's good to be open-minded, and I've approached my whole life from this perspective, rather than the more traditional skeptical close-mindedness that often prevails. So, the big question is this: "Is reincarnation real, and if it is, why do we have to keep coming back?" I can only comment on what I've come up with as a result of studying this fascinating subject and through some of my personal life experiences. That said, I want to share this extraordinary true story about Valerie with you.

One night, Valerie's mom heard her speaking in her bedroom, so she got up to see why her little girl was still awake at such a late hour. To her surprise, she noticed that Valerie was actually sound asleep and was talking in her sleep. As she knelt down to tuck her in once again, she was quite taken aback as she listened to her child speak. There's nothing unusual about talking in one's sleep, so this would be fine, except that Valerie is American — but in this case, she was speaking French!

Valerie was only five and hadn't been exposed to the French language in her young life. As a matter of fact, she was raised in New England in an Italian home. Valerie never knew anything about this incident until many years later when she was grown and her mother mentioned it to her. She asked her mom, "Why did you so readily accept the fact that I was speaking in French?"

In an attempt to rationalize the event to herself, her mother just assumed that Valerie must have heard French from someone or memorized it from the TV. It's typical human nature. We just shake our heads and say, "How funny," or shrug it off, believing that there must be some other logical explanation.

Valerie would have agreed with her mother's reasoning had it been a few words, but according to her mom, she was uttering complete sentences. Her mom explained that she'd continued to speak French in her sleep from time to time until she was ten. It's my belief that in some past life, Valerie had spoken this language fluently. The older she got, the more she integrated into her current life, eventually forgetting her past one. It's interesting that as an adult, she's totally open and truly believes in reincarnation. Doesn't it make sense that Valerie studied French in high school and found the language really easy to learn? She hardly had to study at all!

As a child, I was born with an incredible artistic talent. In fact, I'd win college art contests for my age-group quite frequently and was often called on by teachers and the other students when something needed to be drawn. I loved art and everything about it, and even today I enjoy going to museums and seeing the beautiful canvases and sculptures exhibited. I don't just look at the pictures; I also analyze them — their form and composition — and I try to imagine what technique the artists employed, or how they used color to accentuate what they wanted in their pieces. Sometimes I sit for hours just staring.

If you didn't find me reading as a child, I'd be drawing. I'm not talking about sketching doodles or stick figures . . . I'd be creating my own form of art using all kinds of materials. To me, it didn't matter if it was finger painting, drawing in pencil, or working with charcoal. Once again, like five-year-old Valerie and her French, as a child I never took an art class. Drawing simply came easily and naturally to me.

Is it in my genes? Is there a "good drawer" encoded in my DNA? Or is it that I've been an artist in a previous life? I have to believe that it's the latter — it's not as though my parents or grandparents were artistic. I also believe that when you see children who are born geniuses, whether it's in mathematics, music, or some other area, it's possible that in some way they could still be connected to a past life and inherit part of that talent in this one. Maybe they'll keep that ability if it's trained and used. Kids can choose to acknowledge the gift and hold on to it in this life, or they can let it go as they learn new skills this time around.

According to many of the spiritual practices I've undertaken, the continuity of the soul exists. It's a widely held belief that we reincarnate over and over again to help the progression, evolution, and advancement of our souls. With each lifetime, the soul continues to learn, transform, grow, and evolve as we become more spiritually attuned and grow closer to our Divine Source.

You're the total accumulation of *all* your learning through different lifetimes, and these experiences create the history of your soul. As I've said earlier, your soul is what makes you . . . you. Some of the lessons that you might need to learn in this lifetime may never be dealt with. Equally, there will be those that you attempt to master but may not complete in this lifetime, and they'll most likely be addressed in another one. An unlearned lesson has the tendency to show up even more forcefully the next time until you do in fact get it! The education and progression of the soul doesn't end when you die — it's forever evolving. When you leave this world, you continue to learn and grow on a higher spiritual plane.

I believe that when we leave the spirit world to once again enter into this one, those on the Other Side sadly say good-bye to us; by the same token, when we're born, people on Earth celebrate. When it's our time to pass over, loved ones here mourn, and those on the Other Side now rejoice and welcome us with open arms. I also believe that we reincarnate in what are known as *Soul Groups* — in other words, we return with people whom we've interacted with in previous lifetimes. We often come back as different genders, with alternative roles within a relationship. Our parents now may be our siblings — in a previous life one of them might have been our partner, or they easily could have been our children. How many times have you met a kid who's really playing the role of the parent instead of the child? Is there one brother or sister who, for whatever the reason, you just never got along with, and you're closer to the rest of your siblings? Our lifetimes are a chance for all of us to act out the different roles so that we have a more spiritual understanding from all points of experience.

If you believe in the whole doctrine of reincarnation, it does start to explain why some relationships that we're experiencing feel better than others. Some people elect to be regressed back to a past life in the hope of seeing why they're experiencing a difficult time in this one or to better understand personal-relationship issues. Once they grasp the meaning and the distant root cause of the problem, *then* the real healing process can begin in the present. We all learn through relationships, whether it's the one that we're in now, one from our past, or one from another lifetime.

Past-life recall can assist people who are experiencing specific fears or phobias. For example, if you have a real fear of water and can't swim, you could be regressed back to a previous life where you discover that you drowned. Then you'll understand why you have a fear of water. So too, people who are afraid of flying or high places may discover that they fell to their death in a previous life. Once the cause of the fear or phobia is identified, often the problem is resolved and the conditions vanish. Whether it's swimming in the beautiful ocean, getting on a plane, or being able to visit a skyscraper . . . everything becomes accessible.

Experiencing a past life can be enlightening and enjoyable. If you know someone who's having difficulty here and you believe a past-life regression would be therapeutic, then as long as the person is open, I'd certainly give it a try. However, if you're interested just for curiosity's sake or because you think it might be fun, remember that it's *this* life that should be your main concern; this is the one that's important. What you do today will reflect what you do or don't do in another life, which is most likely why the majority of people don't recall their past lives. My belief is that when you pass over, you leave this physical vessel and go to a higher dimension that vibrates at an elevated frequency, and that's why you don't see it.

When you arrive on the Other Side, you're shown a *life review*, which is exactly that: an opportunity to review your entire life that you just left, including the lessons you learned, as you plan out your next one. As you look back, you experience all the encounters that you've had with others. You also experience every joy, as well as every pain, that you might have caused one another. Each emotion is felt — from the people you've loved or hated to the individual you helped or the one you decided to turn away from. Every interaction is experienced all over again, but this time you're on the receiving end. In a way, you become your own judge and jury. If more people realized this, I believe that there would be less crime and sadness in the world. As souls, we're all connected, so when you hurt someone or strike out at another person, on a spiritual consciousness level you're really hurting yourself, as well as the entire human race.

No matter how many lectures I give, the question of reincarnation always comes up and is often followed by: "If it's true that we reincarnate, then when I die, will my loved ones be there, or will they have already reincarnated back on Earth?" Remember that my opinion is purely my own, and it's not the only point of view. The answer I usually give is this: I don't believe that we're constantly recycled immediately like in a factory . . . there could be many years between lives. I do feel that as a soul you have free will and the opportunity to come right back if you choose.

Time has no meaning in the spiritual world; it's humankind who made up the concept of linear time. I also appreciate the explanation I heard my colleague and fellow medium Gordon Smith give, which likens reincarnation to how computers work — namely, that there are many levels and dimensions to our soul. When we come here, we're playing out a certain program (or multiple programs) from our hard drive, which is our entire, or whole, soul. The soul experiencing this lifetime is just a piece of that bigger one. So when the program that's you eventually passes away, it will go back into the whole soul, into the hard drive, and it will always be there along with your loved ones. I know that it's kind of deep, but it does resonate with me and make sense.

If you're seriously considering investigating a past life, then please find a reputable practitioner. I've worked closely with Brian Weiss, M.D., the author of the bestseller *Many Lives, Many Masters;* and his Website recommends practitioners throughout the world whom he's trained. Understanding that the soul's journey is never ending gives us all the hope that it's never too late to learn, that we do have choices for our soul's growth as we experience everything with our time here, and that we have free will as to how we want to live it.

If you could stop time for a brief moment and take a look back, would you say that you're watching life or participating in it? Ask yourself the following two questions: (1) *Did I accomplish what I set out to do?* and (2) *Whom did I help?* I believe that when it's your time to go over to the Other Side, you'll be asked these questions. If you can answer them positively, then I feel that it will have been all worthwhile.

Soul Wounds

We're all deliberate players with respect to how we live, love, and learn and the way we shape our lives. Every soul that chooses to be born into this incarnation will have its own unique blueprint; and encoded within it are all our gifts, talents, and abilities, as well as the lessons that we need to learn. The lessons that make the greatest impact, those we remember most, have a tendency to be the painful ones.

Earlier in this book, I discussed how your special talents assist you in being all that you can be. Most people don't realize that pain can be a powerful teacher of wisdom and knowledge for your soul, as well as for those you touch through your lifetime. Your gifts, talents, and abilities, along with your joys and hurts, will make up who you really are and who you'll become, helping you live a life in full alignment with your purpose. The difficult experiences of life are just as valuable as the joyous ones.

We've all experienced suffering in our lifetime. Sometimes it quickly fades away to become a distant memory, while on other occasions it remains with you as though it only happened yesterday. This pain could have been formed at almost any time in your life, from your childhood to your later years. Similarly, it could be a carryover from a previous lifetime. No matter what caused the hurt — whether it was an issue of love and the heart, being exposed to negative behavior over a period of time, or even witnessing pain as I did as a young child — it can leave a scar or imprint on your soul. These are known as *soul wounds*. I considered including this section in Chapter 5, "The Healer Within," but I wanted to show you how pain can help you on your soul's journey through this lifetime.

You very likely have one main soul wound, and knowing what it is will help you find one of the gifts or talents that you were meant to share with the world. A single soul wound can easily encompass other issues that you feel emotional or passionate about. On a personal note, I've mentioned that I grew up in an alcoholic home. I don't go around looking for pity, but constantly witnessing ugly scenes and the pain that they caused has provided me with some really useful tools to help others cope with similar situations. In this case, my suffering is someone else's salvation.

The good news is that I've moved on with my life, forgiven my father, and released the anger, enabling my soul to heal, advance, and grow. I now use this special soul wound to assist and heal others. Not only do I help people through my mediumship, but I also support special children's charities and women's shelters, and I do all that I can for those who grew up with a similar background. This soul wound, which could have easily taken me down a negative path in my life, has enhanced my soul and who I am. As I reached adulthood, I decided that rather than just moan about my situation and upbringing, it was up to me to do something about it. Each and every one of us will have a wound that affects us in different ways. Some people heal and move on, while others choose to ignore their hurt.

Unfortunately, we're in what I like to refer to as the *numbing society*. We have a tendency to numb ourselves in an attempt to deaden our pain. When we don't let it out, however, *nothing* can get out, including all the love and goodness that our soul wants to bring forth. We numb ourselves in various ways — through alcohol, drugs, and abusive relationships, for instance, or by becoming a workaholic — so that we can simply *not* feel. When it comes to the wounds of the soul, don't ignore them . . . embrace them, learn their valuable lessons, and integrate them so that they can benefit you and your life as you continue to move forward.

In my first book, *Born Knowing*, I introduced Victoria and her beautiful daughter Quimby, who passed away in a tragic amusement-park accident. For Victoria, losing her only child was *her* soul wound. I can't imagine a greater pain than what a parent feels when he or she loses a child, but Victoria's story is a true inspiration to others, as she went on to help many other children and parents. After Quimby (the Swedish word for "lifesaving") passed away, Victoria took her painful loss and used it to help change the amusement-park safety laws that were clearly inadequate at the time and needed updating. I believe that Quimby really was given that name for a reason. Think of how many lives have now been saved due to Quimby's death.

A friend of Victoria's who lost her daughter to an eating disorder now lectures throughout schools to young people and parents in order to spread awareness of the dangers of this type of disease. When you use your pain to help others, you're healing the wound as well as yourself. In the cases of both Victoria and her friend, the pain of losing a child helped them express love, compassion, and courage through giving and using their gifts. They're living their purpose of aiding and healing others and being all that they can be — a true reflection of God, the Divine Source.

Shamanic practices also deal with what's known as *psychic wounds* of the soul. Shamans believe that when people experience an emotional or traumatic event, they could lose a piece of their soul. Their soul is temporarily incomplete and their destiny is then slightly off course. Through the practice of *soul retrieval,* the shaman is able to recover the pieces that were splintered off at the time of the traumatic occurrence, enabling them to become whole again and continue their desired destiny.

You may be asking yourself, *Do I have a "soul wound," and how do I know what it is?* A soul wound will be at the very core of your existence. It can be quite ingenious, often placing you in certain situations or manifesting a particular theme that keeps playing out in your life so that you can address it and start to heal. It's almost like going to the same play over and over again, but while the plot remains the same, the players are different. For example, it could be an abusive relationship. If people keep choosing that type of relationship, then they must learn the lesson that they deserve better . . . they need to honor themselves. Once that's understood and the healing and recovery has been accomplished, they can go on to help others, which is always their choice.

Soul wounds have a tendency to flare up when you're around similar people who've confronted the same issue or pain that you're experiencing. You may be watching the evening news and find yourself suddenly enraged by a story that sounds all too familiar to you. Once a soul wound is addressed and dealt with, healing can begin. This doesn't mean that it will be gone and forgotten: Just like a cut that forms a scar, your wound leaves its own mark to remind you and to move you in a more positive direction. Pain doesn't have to define you, but it can be a powerful transformational antidote when applied correctly. Most important, though, it's what you do about it that matters. Learn, grow, and honor your pain. It's become part of your soul's essence, and if you allow it, it can become a powerful and motivating source guiding you toward the next step you take on your journey.

Wake-Up Calls

Hello? It's God calling. Anyone listening? Often when we don't heed our intuition — the language of the soul — or when obvious synchronicities aren't grabbing our attention, we'll receive what I refer to as *Wake-Up Calls*. Usually they have a tendency to be pretty loud so that we *do* pay attention and act. I often mention in my lectures that the Universe has a clever way of kicking us in the ass to move us along or put us back on our correct path. But, of course, as rational humans, when we receive a Wake-Up Call, we try to explain it away or concoct some other logical explanation. Doing so might sway those around us, but the call will only come again . . . this time even louder!

I had my own Wake-Up Call some years ago. It was the time of my car accident in Los Angeles. I was living the fast life that so many of us get caught up in. I was always out and partying, worked a job that I hated, and remained in a relationship that should have ended months earlier. I was just barely 30, living carefree and often carelessly. Like so many young people in L.A., I thought that's what it was all about. As the months slipped by, signs started appearing, telling me to pay attention: Friends were suggesting that I slow down, my family was wondering why I hadn't called, bills were beginning to pile up, and the feelings of stagnation that I'd ignored were surfacing. My life started to feel out of kilter. I was offered new opportunities, but I turned them away in the belief that they were simply not for me, or I made up some other excuse. I turned a deaf ear to my soul's voice and pretended not to see all the red flags that were being hoisted around me.

Well, little did I know it, but I was about to get my big kick in the ass! The accident happened when I was coming home from work one evening after putting in a double shift. It was late — I was tired, and the weather was awful, too, just to make matters worse. The accident was very traumatic; I could have died, but I was lucky enough to walk away. When it happened, I knew that this was *my* Wake-Up Call . . . and this time, I chose to listen. I'd already had a few lesser Wake-Up Calls in my life, but I was aware that if I didn't heed the warnings of this one, *I'd* be the one on the Other Side talking through a medium to friends and family here. I knew that I had to change my life and pull myself together. I felt a bit like an actor waiting to go onstage who hears: "This is your last and final call." I'd just gotten mine!

We all get these special calls. Stop and think for a moment. Can you remember when you had one (or more than one)? Yes? Something comes to your mind at once, doesn't it? Wake-Up Calls aren't intended to be punishments . . . they're meant for you to immediately stop and look at your life. They're telling you that it's time to make some changes and get back in alignment with what's for the highest good of you as well as your soul. These calls are really giving you an opportunity to start over again, a chance for a whole new beginning. I can't emphasize this strongly enough: Don't ignore them!

Sometimes it *does* take a drastic change to truly begin living! When the accident woke me up, I began to review my life and make the appropriate modifications. I left the relationship that *John* had gotten lost in and moved out on my own. All I had when I left was a round rattan chair and my clothes in a few cardboard boxes. My new apartment — which was on the other side of the city — was cheap and my landlord did nothing, so it was up to me to fix it up. I was okay with everything, because for the first time in my life, it was totally mine and I had to fend for myself.

My life immediately started to change. I was paying my bills on time. People whom I thought were friends fell by the wayside, as I realized that in reality, they were just part-time companions or acquaintances. I tuned in to my soul for answers the way I used to when I was a child. The intuitive psychic abilities that I had then were back, except this time they were so much stronger. This one very loud Wake-Up Call is what put me back on the path that my soul began so many years ago. Thankfully, I'd started the slow process of transformation toward becoming the real me.

Wake-Up Calls can come in any number of forms and from different sources. They could be from a relative, friend, or stranger — or from a traumatic event, a book, a dream, or even a health issue. Awhile ago I saw my neighbor Barbara at the post office, and I asked how she and her husband were. She told me that she was fine but that they should have been in Florida. Well, of course that was an open invitation to ask why they *weren't* there but were home instead. We walked outside, and she related the whole story to me.

Barbara and her husband, Frank, had planned a much-needed vacation to visit friends and family. They ran a sizable property-development business, and although it was successful, it had been a long and strenuous year. They'd built dozens of new homes and took real pride in them. They were quite excited as they sat on the plane with just an hour to go before landing in Florida. As the aircraft started its descent, Frank suddenly felt a sharp pang in his chest. He was obviously in severe pain and was struggling to breathe. Barbara called over a flight attendant. Minutes later, the pilot, deciding it was safer to get Frank off the plane and to a hospital, chose to make an emergency landing at the first opportunity.

Frank was rushed to the hospital. After a thorough examination in the emergency room, the doctor told the couple that Frank had come very close to a heart attack without actually having one. Apparently, the change of air pressure in the cabin had triggered warning signs that he had heart problems. Being on that plane actually saved Frank from an imminent heart attack. He went on to have triple-bypass surgery. This Wake-Up Call saved his life and sent out a loud message that he desperately needed to change his lifestyle.

I just recently saw Barbara again, and she told me that Frank has in fact made the choice to change his life. He's no longer the first one on the job at 5 A.M., and when his body is telling him to slow down and rest more, he does. Frank is now taking time each day to notice everything and everyone close to his heart and to make sure that they know it. I'd say he's off to a great new life!

Wake-Up Calls can happen at any time, and I believe that before you incarnated, some were preplanned by you and your guides to occur at certain points in your life, almost as if you said, "I'm going to place a Wake-Up Call when I reach the age of 30 to move me in a different direction." These calls are personal and are only meant for you. If you think back to a time when you believe that you received one, you should be able to understand why you did and what it meant.

You don't need a lot of training to recognize a spiritual Wake-Up Call. They are, as I've said, loud and usually quite obvious. If something happens to you that makes you realize how lucky you were to safely get out of a situation and you promise yourself, *I'll never do that again,* then that, my friend, is a Wake-Up Call. When one occurs, you have the opportunity to address something in your life or reconsider a certain direction that you were about to take. Hopefully, when you receive your own personal Wake-Up Call (and trust me — you will), you'll stop for a moment and answer it with an open awareness. Above all, be willing to act sooner rather than later. The Divine Source is always looking out for you, and It makes every attempt to keep you moving forward on your soul's journey.

Temple of the Soul

No matter how hard you may try to change this fact, you're born with one body in this lifetime. It may be thin, fat, small, large, toned, short, or tall — whatever the shape, color, or size, you only get one. It's yours forever, so accept it, embrace it . . . and above all, honor it. The precious vehicle that we call the body is the way that your soul expresses itself and gets from place to place on its journey here in this dense, molecular physical dimension. Most people can't stand the body they were born with. Some perfect it with exercise combined with a good, healthy lifestyle, while others choose to surgically change it. If we could only see through the eyes of the Divine how beautiful we are, we'd know and recognize it for what it truly is — a wondrous temple for the soul.

The body is a miracle in itself, and used properly, it can be a wonderful intuitive resource for tapping into the power of the soul. Your body is your soul's instrument to show the outside world the luminous light that emanates from within. It's easy to tell when people are really happy, as they just glow from the inside out. The light truly radiates from them, and it's a joy to step into their space and their aura and bask in their positive energy. Think of the number of times someone has said, "You're beaming!" The body and soul are constantly striving to live, work, and journey through this life in ideal harmony. They dance together as though they were always meant to partner with each other.

The *body* is the physical vessel that the soul uses to reach out and experience the outside world, just as the *soul* is the means by which the body transcends, understands, and encounters spiritual experiences. In the developed world, we live in a society that's forever rushing — always push, push, push . . . go, go, go! Our technology has totally surpassed our spirituality. We so rarely take the time to pause long enough to become aware of the beautiful details all around us. It's the little things that are easily missed in our hurried physical lives that can have such a profound effect on our souls.

Now that I've been a medium for more than 17 years, I've been privileged to share boundless joy as well as sorrow, and I continually hear stories of missed opportunities from the thousands of people I come into contact with, whether they're here among the living or on the Other Side. As a result, I encourage others — and I still remind myself — to stop and be present and mindful of what's inside as well as around each and every one of us. Again, I offer the most obvious advice: "Do something about it now while you're still here."

Even when I drink a cup of tea, I savor the moment. I bring in and use all my physical senses as I relish this aromatic liquid, and I use the gentle sipping motion as a form of meditation to spend some quiet reflective time in the temple of my soul. I hold the mug of tea in both my palms, smelling its sweet aroma and looking at it with mindfulness. I take a sip, swallow slowly, and inhale before gently breathing out. I imagine the people who picked the tea leaves so that I may more fully enjoy my beverage. I drink my tea in the here and now, in the present, and I say to myself: *I am alive — I am a soul — I am a miracle.*

It goes without saying that if you want to keep your body in good health, you should have a balanced diet, get plenty of rest, and take the appropriate vitamins to keep it in top form. At the beginning of this book, I likened the body, soul, and spirit to an automobile. The exterior of the car is your physical body, your soul is the driver, and the gas that fuels your body is your spirit. Every 5,000 miles or so, the vehicle (your body) needs its regular service so that its continued journey will be smooth.

I received an unexpected "tune-up" recently while attending a talk at my favorite local bookstore, Circles of Wisdom, in Andover, Massachusetts. There was a young man there named Joseph Carringer, who was giving a fascinating lecture on how sound is one of humanity's greatest healing sources for realigning, restoring, and revitalizing the body. He explained how he became a professional didgeridoo player and actually perfected his ability by studying the Aborigines in Australia. A didgeridoo (pronounced *did-jer-i-doo*) is a musical instrument consisting of a long, thick wooden pipe that the player blows, creating a deep, reverberating, almost mesmerizing sound. It's believed that the spirit world gave the didgeridoo to the Aborigines to act as a portal from this world to the next.

I find the whole idea of using sound for the body and soul fascinating. Quantum physicists have theorized that the smallest particles in our bodies are not actually particles at all, but instead are sound-like waveforms that hold the larger particles and atoms together. These waveforms appear to have a frequency similar to that of the Sanskrit "om." I really believe that the Universe has a rhythm, if people would simply stop and listen.

Now, there are many ways to shift and move your soul, but what I experienced that evening at Circles of Wisdom took my breath away. You've heard the expression "Feel the vibration," right? Well, the vibrations I felt when Joseph practiced Harmonic Therapy on me that evening was pure *sounding* for my soul. He had me lie on a mesh cot, and while he played the didgeridoo and aimed it at my body, I felt my energy centers (chakras) begin to pulsate as energetic waves of sound ran up and down my spine. My body (my vehicle) and my soul came alive with a resonance that I felt almost matched that of the Universe. It was truly an awesome experience!

For days before I walked into the bookstore, I had lower-back pain that refused to go away, but after the treatment, it just evaporated. Joseph explained that Harmonic Therapy could be used to aid in meditation and relaxation, acting as a tuning fork for your body's natural resonant vibration on a cellular level. Reported effects of the therapy range from relief of muscle pain and stress to a greater sense of clarity and a heightened energy flow along reopened chakra points. The best part is that it's noninvasive, totally painless, and so enjoyable.

Whether you use meditation, music, sound, or your own personal mantra to enter your temple, always remember to look upon your body as a miracle. I constantly remind my students and readers of one very important statement, which I want to repeat: "The same material that makes up the Universe is inside you." You need not look beyond your own body for heaven, because it's a state of being, in a sense, and not necessarily a location somewhere out in the cosmos.

Honor and take care of your temple — you only get one in this lifetime — and it will serve you and your soul quite well in the journey we call life.

Respect Others' Beliefs

When you travel a spiritual path, it's not uncommon for you to feel alone. After all, it's your path and no one else's. But it's important to remember that there are like-minded souls out there. I recommend that you reach out and investigate different groups and organizations that feel right. Even when you don't consciously do so, you may find that people of the same vibrational level will be attracted to you. Hopefully, you'll still have the opportunity to spiritually bond with one another. It's a wonderful thing when you share your experiences, because not only are you conveying what you've learned or experienced, you're letting your soul educate others and express itself. The whole process can be quite liberating.

You're on your spiritual path, so please honor the fact that it's meant for *you*. You shouldn't try to drag, pull, bribe, or coerce anyone else into believing what you feel is true for yourself. One of my favorite sayings is: "Everyone is exactly where they are supposed to be." I feel that you have your own unique path to take as you journey through this life, and it's nobody else's job to move you away from it. If you were to exert undue pressure to make someone agree with your views, it could result in your taking them further away from their own journey. It's the journey of the soul in this life where you learn some of the most poignant lessons. When you respect and honor the beliefs of others, it will ensure that you're not leading them away from the lessons that their soul needs to learn.

Many people at my lectures and workshops often ask me, "John, what can I do to make someone I care about understand and accept what I believe in?" I try to explain that walking a spiritual path is very personal to each individual — it's all about free will and choice. Usually it helps when one person balances out the other. For example, I know that I wouldn't want to live with another me. Could you envision spending your life with another you? Probably not! If you have a passion for metaphysics and really believe in its teachings but your partner or spouse has no interest, then there could still be a benefit. In truth, the other person may very well be a grounding force for you. You, in turn, may show him or her a new way of looking at something. When the time is right, others around you may begin to question things outside themselves, and hopefully, they'll also look inward to find their own answers. You may even be the catalyst to boost their vibrational level, enabling them to see even greater opportunity and beauty. I guess there's something to the saying "Opposites attract."

When you take those early steps in your spiritual development, you may notice that some of the people in your life step back or disappear completely. This doesn't mean that you've developed an ego or that you're better all of a sudden. It's more about the fact that your consciousness and vibration is stepping up a level. When this happens, those around you who don't match your frequency have a tendency to draw back or fall away. This doesn't have to be a bad thing, since people are exactly where they're supposed to be and you have to respect that. What's happening at this time is the universal law of bringing others into your life who match your vibration. I really recommend that you stay grounded during the whole process of spiritual development. Once again, don't forget that you're a spiritual being having physical experiences. Honor all of you.

CHAPTER EIGHT

Soul Living

I f you want to tap into the power of the soul and live a life of passion and potential, then you first have to remember that you *are* a soul here and now. I find it ironic that we come from a place of Divine Source and inspiration, yet so many of us spend the duration of our lives trying to find it again! When you acknowledge that you're a soul and not just a body, then there's really no limit to what you can achieve. Once you begin *living* and *viewing* the world from a soul level and you start to recognize the nature and workings of its spiritual power, you'll have a higher perspective and a deeper understanding of your purpose and life, along with the world and everyone in it.

Throughout these pages, I've taught you about:

- Understanding the soul

- How to use and trust your soul sense of intuition

- How the power and energy of love is vital to your soul's well-being

- Ways to help heal yourself as well as others

- Methods to break free of the past so that your soul can learn, grow, and above all, evolve

Your journey doesn't stop when you finish this book, for in reality it's just begun. This is your chance right now to take on the responsibility of owning your power and living as the Divine soul that you are. I don't want you to say that you'll start tomorrow or the next day or tell yourself, *I'll do it when I have time.* Today is the day . . . now is the moment. Once you realize that you can access the phenomenal internal database called wisdom anytime you wish, it becomes an empowering motivator to begin living the life you were meant to live. A great way to start is by acknowledging and repeating: "I am a soul." When you say these words, your soul resonates with what you're expressing, and your consciousness expands even more. There will be times throughout your life when for any number of reasons you may unconsciously pull away from your soul. The constant process of reminding yourself that you're more than this physical being will bring you back to your soul's awareness. You'll feel the effect as you make that connection.

To live from your soul is a commitment and an ongoing spiritual practice. It can sometimes be challenging when the outside world is so deafening that it literally muffles your soul's inner voice of wisdom. Many people ask me how they can become more spiritual. I wish that there were a quick and easy answer to this all-too-common question. You don't suddenly acquire such a quality by taking a workshop or reading a book. It's not something that can be packaged up into a neat parcel by someone else; rather, it's a total way of being.

Everything that you do in your life can be spiritual. How you treat yourself, others, and the earth; acts of generosity and compassion; and giving and receiving unconditional love are all part of being spiritual. There's no one way to go about it, nor are there any quick fixes to becoming enlightened. It's both a process and a journey at the same time.

No matter who you are, where you've been, or what you've done, you always have the freedom of choice to begin leading a spiritual life — to start living from the soul. You may be saying, "But I really wasn't nice to people," or "I've led such a bad life." Whether you've had the life of a tyrant or an angel, you're still a soul, and you always will be. As such, you have a piece of God, the

Divine Source, inside you at all times . . . it's a package deal. Because you're human, you have a soul and possess all the power that goes with it. Your soul doesn't discriminate, exclude, or condemn; and no matter how much you may ignore it, perhaps at times even abandoning it, it will never leave you. All your soul asks is that you turn to it and be open and receptive to its Divine wisdom — after all, it only wants what's best for you and your highest good.

Your Life, Your Choice

Wherever you are right now, at this precise time in your life you're there because you took yourself there. Yes, it's all about *you!* Every decision you've made brought you to this very point. I do believe that *some* events in your life are fated to happen, but you have free will — the choice in the moment to determine what you do and how you respond when these events occur. As a soul, you're an accumulation of all your experiences that are taking place now, as well as those from the past. The choices that you make with respect to these experiences shape the quality of how you're going to live your life. I mentioned earlier that after I had that accident in Los Angeles, I let it become a positive experience for me. I believe that it was meant to happen, and it was up to my free will to either complain and blame the world or seize the opportunity and use it to wake myself up so that I could enhance my life.

There are many different roads you may decide to take on your soul's journey. When your soul incarnates here in the physical world, its predestined voyage will bring you from point A to point B. It's always your choice to pick the route that you want to travel, which will determine how fast you get there. You may take a quick, direct route from point A to point B, *or* you might meander through different side roads, experiencing all that life has to offer as you take your time getting to your soul's ultimate destination.

Sometimes other people can influence or accelerate our course or throw us off it altogether. We often have a tendency to listen to others, especially when we trust them. They love to tell us what they think is the preferred direction we should be going in.

If you're going to seek advice, *please* do your homework and find the person who's best equipped to help you make the most informed decisions. If you receive feedback from someone who's less qualified and it's not the best advice, it's easy to blame the person — but in reality, it was *your* choice to listen to that individual's opinion. Ultimately, everything really does come down to the simple premise that you're held accountable for the conditions around you. Blaming others takes away from your soul's energy, and when you assume responsibility for your decisions and your life, your soul can't help but become empowered.

In my book *Born Knowing,* I talked about one of my first psychic teachers, my friend Vincent J. Barra. I remember years ago when I'd call him and complain about something that was happening in my life, he had this uncanny knack for always putting the responsibility back on me by saying, "So what are *you* going to do about it, John?" I always respected that about him. He'd never offer the answers but instead would empower me to reach inside and get them for myself. He did more for me than he'll ever know.

As a soul, you're quite capable of manifesting your own reality and your own future. You need to be more conscious of your feelings (negative or positive), thoughts, beliefs, and actions . . . it all matters. When you take on the responsibility for being more aware, you'll feel a sense of empowerment in the knowledge that you can change whatever you want in your life. Once you understand that you have free will, it puts your soul firmly in the driver's seat to decide which direction you want to take. Every choice determines if you're going to be moving closer or farther away from your purpose.

When I think back, I like to see how the choices in my life brought me to this point. If I'd never made the decision to move to California, which is where I had my automobile accident that put me on this path, would I still have somehow walked the same one? . . . Who knows? I believe that my point B was about being a psychic medium, but it was my choice to decide the correct route to take to get here.

You have to stop and ask yourself questions once in a while to check in with yourself and see where you are at this point on your soul's journey. If you're moving farther away from where you want to be, then inquire: *What do I need to do right now to put me back on my path?* At least by asking, you're taking on the responsibility for your own life's direction. Sometimes it's good to let go at the river's edge and allow the flow of life to take you where you're supposed to be. It can be quite liberating when you do. Sometimes the opportunities and choices suddenly become exciting but you still feel safe in surrendering the outcome. Other times, though, it makes more sense to grab a pair of oars and steer yourself in a certain direction. Your choice comes from your own free will — hang on or let go? At least you're asking yourself the questions that will assist your soul in answering you and telling you what it wants and needs.

Tips for Making Better Choices

— When you take responsibility for your life and the choices you make, you begin to tap into the power of your soul. You'll be able to listen to the intuitive wisdom that's *inside* you and apply it to your *outside* world. Next time you make a decision, stop for a moment and ask yourself, *How do I feel about this decision? Does it feel positive or negative, and why?* Simply by doing so, you'll be accessing your own intuition and be guided toward better choices. By making smarter, more considered ones, you'll no longer be a victim of circumstance and will have the power and ability to change your outcome.

— It's always *your* choice as to what kind of day you want to have. Even before your foot touches the floor, try smiling — you don't need a reason. Just as a result of this simple act, you'll begin your day in a positive way. It will even send a spark of upliftment into your aura, which will help put *you* in an upbeat mood. All thought creates reality, so by starting off in this way, more positive vibes and opportunities will be attracted to you. Once again, you might as well enjoy the day. After all, you gave up 24 hours of your life for it, right?

— Intuition can be an excellent resource to assist you in making decisions. Here's another technique that you may want to try. Imagine two roads in front of you with individual signs representing each decision. Take your time as you walk down each one and observe all the surroundings — notice everything. Do you feel positive or negative? Are the roads rugged or smooth? Is the landscape rich with greenery, or is it barren? Use this technique for small decisions at first as you build your intuition and confidence.

— You should choose from the heart. If I'm having difficulty understanding someone, I try to look beyond what I'm seeing in front of me. Layer upon layer of life's issues may be covering the goodness that's inside that individual. People will also put up a front as a form of protective armor because they were hurt in the past. I choose to feel that they have a kind, pure heart. I opt to look for the good that's in every person and situation. It may not be easy at times, but at least I try.

— At some time or other, we've all made bad choices in our lives. Hopefully, we learn from them, try not to repeat them, and move on. Making peace with a poor decision from the past will help you toward more positive future ones. Decide right now, at this very moment, to strive to make better choices in the future. By making this simple resolution, you're telling yourself and your soul that you will be all that you can be. Choose wisely and the regrets will be few.

Stepping into Your Power

It's true: We're such mighty beings and we don't even realize it. To accept that we're a Divine extension of God, a soul with unbelievable power, is one of the bravest leaps any of us can take in this life. It's a power that's our birthright, yet we often turn away from it, refusing to acknowledge it or even learn how to tap into it, which prevents us from being all that we can be. There are any number of possible reasons for this, such as fearing the judgment of others, being afraid of failure or success, or following someone else's opinion of what's best for us. Many of us simply want to play it safe and decide to stay right where we are. As you reach the end of this book, you'll appreciate why I love this famous quote by T. S. Eliot: "Only those who will risk going too far can possibly find out how far one can go."

You can actually see, feel, and experience this power when it's infusing your soul. It often manifests and builds when you start using your talents, gifts, and abilities to bring about change in your life as well as those of others. Not so long ago I remember watching a celebrity on television talking about a charity that he clearly felt deeply about and generously sponsored. As he was speaking, you could see his soul in its true form, almost like a luminous entity of light — he was beaming from the inside out. When I witness this energetic power manifesting throughout someone's being, I refer to it as *soul shine.*

When I talk about power, I'm referring to the personal power that's within us all. You may identify it as a spiritual force, an energy, or personal magnetism. Whatever you decide to call it, it's yours to acknowledge, honor, and use. We all have this power, but sadly, we either choose not to harness it or are too afraid to do so. While I was studying to be a medium in England, I did extensive research, read all the books I could get my hands on, meditated, sat in a spiritual-development circle every week for two years, attended workshops and schools, and even learned from other professional mediums. After all this training, my friends, teachers, and fellow mediums said that I was ready to do the work that my soul was meant to do. It was as though it were my soul's destiny.

Of course, I kept telling myself that somehow I wasn't prepared. In a way, I felt like an actor who constantly takes drama classes yet never gets up on the stage. I knew for a fact that I wasn't going to move forward unless I worked on letting go of the past. I had to build my self-esteem so that I could finally honor and step into my power.

A big part of stepping into your power is the whole process of loving and accepting yourself. By doing so, you're actually embracing and appreciating the *whole* of you. Just as in my own past, many people feel that they have to be different or improve themselves before they can begin living in their power. Sometimes it's as simple as showing up and saying that you're ready to do the work. It doesn't matter where you are in your life. Come as you are! We're all the same. Bring your baggage — arrive with your past, along with all your faults, emotions, and drama. If you're willing to put in the effort and make the commitment to improving yourself and growing as a soul, then you've just taken the most important *action* — your first step.

One evening a teacher in England taught me a valuable lesson that I've never forgotten. It was just before I was about to demonstrate my mediumship in front of a large class of fellow students. I was quite anxious since I was only a fledgling. My teacher, who I knew would be joining me onstage, clearly sensed my nervous tension. She leaned over to me and said in her quiet voice, "John, the reason you'll be up there tonight isn't to be judged, but to trust and work for spirit." I clambered onto the stage and nervously stared out at the sea of faces in front of me.

I realize that most people don't know that when we mediums step up there, we *never* know what's going to happen. We must simply get out of our own way and have total trust in the spirit world. No two demonstrations are ever the same, and we must have faith that we'll be successful in linking this world with the next in order to deliver the messages from those on the Other Side. Even to this day, some 17 years later, they've never let me down.

That evening, after taking my teacher's advice, I accepted myself by honoring that I had in fact "done the work" that earned me the right to be up there onstage. I stopped worrying about other people's judgments. It was one of those life-changing moments . . . I truly experienced the strength of my soul's power start to transform my life. I felt as though my new purpose was being born, and I was destined to touch as many souls as I could with my ability.

Before the night was over, my teacher gave me one more tip on harnessing and honoring my power. Her advice can be used in all areas of life where you need a little inner strength, from public speaking in front of larger audiences to dealing with a sensitive issue with an individual. This is what my teacher recommended:

Imagine that you're stepping into a big circle. As you stand in the middle of it, know that you have every right to be in that ring of power. If you've done the work, then you deserve to be there in *your* circle — this is your time and your space. Somehow just imagining that you're standing there gives your soul the confidence to step forward.

EXERCISE 1: Stepping into Your Power — Honoring the Self

Action equals power. Taking just one simple step toward discovering the limitless potential of your soul is the beginning of being all that you can be. I took vital action to see where my soul was leading me when I moved to England to study the mechanics of mediumship. Had I not acted so decisively, who knows what I'd be doing now or where I'd be?

This exercise will help *you* take the first steps in accepting and appreciating the whole of you:

1. Close your eyes and breathe deeply and slowly. I want you to think back to a time when you did a good deed for someone. Visualize that scene playing out in your mind . . . really see it. If you're having a hard time picturing the event, then stay with the memory of it for a few moments. Once you've connected with it, feel the emotions that are attached to the recollection of doing that good deed. Remember the way you felt about yourself at the time and how the other person responded after you performed the act of kindness. Notice how this emotion makes you feel inside, and observe how your soul seems illuminated. Remain with this feeling for a while. Let it sink into your consciousness as you accept and know that you're a warm, loving, and compassionate soul.

2. Now, in your mind, I want you to take this same feeling and bring it to any area in your life that you think needs attention. Is there a certain direction or action that you hope to take? Do you want to work on your spirituality? Does your soul need caring for? Is there a concern in your relationship that you want to address?

Is there a health problem you should focus on? Take one issue at a time. Ask your soul how you can improve the part of your life that you're concentrating on. What action do you need to take?

You may get an immediate response, or an answer might not be forthcoming. Trust that it will arrive, even though it may not show up in the way you want or expect it to. Synchronicity plays a big part when you begin to live your life from a soul level, so watch for those all-important signs and incidents that just appear out of the blue. Equally, you may want to work on a certain area of your life but your soul might have other plans, bringing up a totally different issue than the one you were thinking of. Remember that you don't always get what you want, but you usually get what you need.

3. Stay with that same energy from the good deed, and see the particular area in your life that you just selected. Now I want you to *feel* it improving bit by bit, eventually visualizing it fully resolved, positive, and healthy. Believe that you're special and that you're truly unique and meant to be happy. Throughout this book, I've explained about the effects of positive affirmations, especially when infused with emotion. I'd like you to say the following affirmations and repeat them three times a day. You may even want to post them somewhere where they're visible. Here they are:

I am soul.
I have unlimited potential.
I now step into my power, and I appreciate all of me.
The Divine Source flows in me, through me, and from me.
I can achieve anything I want.
I now know myself as I really am.
I own my power.
I am power.

4. Finish this exercise by letting your positive emotion soak into your whole being and through your aura. Finally, try to extend it out as far as you can. Take this feeling into every day, week, and part of your life. When you step into your own power, you're also accepting your truth that you're a Divine soul — one that wants

you to be all that you can be and that has the ability to affect the world in ways you may never have thought possible.

EXERCISE 2: Seeing the Divine

Many years ago I was taught this exercise that will really assist you in overcoming those feelings of loneliness. It can help to realize that you have a connection to something far greater than yourself. You are, and always will be, connected to God — the Divine Source. When you begin to appreciate and live at this soul level, you'll know that you're never alone . . . but more important, you'll realize just how powerful you really are.

When I first practiced this exercise, I remember thinking, *How easy could this be?* Well, I was wrong — it took commitment and focus to achieve the full benefits. I've never forgotten the lesson that it taught me, so I want you to try it, too. Afterward, you may experience a total shift in your spiritual perception.

First, I want you to choose just one day this week to practice it. It doesn't matter which day it is, although I recommend earlier in the week; that way, your energy is at its peak, as opposed to at the end, when you're often exhausted.

From the time you set your feet on the floor in the morning until the time you finally get off of them in the evening, I want you to see everyone as a soul. When you look in your mirror first thing in the morning, practice viewing yourself as a Divine expression of God. Then I want you to perceive every single person you come into contact with during the day — yes, everyone — as a Divine soul. Don't necessarily look at the physical body standing in front of you; rather, use your imagination and your spiritual eyes to view the *soul light.*

When I do this exercise, I like to imagine that there's a tiny light that's visible to me in the heart center of all the people I meet. Once I see that soul radiance, everything else about them seems to magically open up. In reality, what happens is that the energy between us blends as we make a soul-to-soul connection. It's extraordinary . . . it's as though I've known them for far longer than just that moment in time.

This exercise isn't as easy as it sounds, but it's so worth it. Your consciousness will begin to expand, and you'll notice that you have a different perception and a renewed appreciation of other people, as well as yourself and your life. I find the following prayer helpful when reaching out to God, as well as people, on soul level.

Divinity Prayer

May the goodness in me
acknowledge the goodness in you.
May the goodness in you
acknowledge the goodness in me.

Checking In and Tuning Up

If we're going to live from our soul, then we have to listen to its wisdom. As a psychic and a medium, I believe that most of the drama in our lives manifests when we don't act in accordance with our inner guidance. Our soul knows what it wants and needs. If we're not in alignment with it, then we can become off balance, and the outside world then manifests what's happening to us on the inside.

There will be times in your life when your soul is screaming out to you, and the thoughts resound loudly in your head: *What am I doing? I really should get a grip on my life! I can't keep living in this way!* When you find yourself grappling with these questions, it's usually during a particularly busy, emotional, or traumatic time in your life. This is a big clue that your soul is trying to get your attention.

I call these moments *Soul Cry-Outs.* Your soul is yelling at you, saying, "Hey! I'm here and you haven't paid any attention to me at all lately! I *can* help!" At times such as these, it will send up signals to your psychic and physical senses, depositing markers along the way that can even appear in your dreams. The power of the soul has no boundaries, and I believe that meeting strangers who somehow bring hidden messages with them isn't an accident. Your *inner* guidance can summon a thought or action, or even manifest a situation in your *outside* life, to get you to *stop* and think about what's happening right in front of you. Next time this occurs and you're faced with a decision, try asking yourself: *What would God and my soul want me to do?*

In the society we live in, it's easy to get caught up in the day-to-day routine, adopting the same schedule over and over. We pull away from the Source that fills our soul, which only exacerbates the feeling of being tired, drained, or confused. It's easy to become immersed in our work, caring for someone who's sick, or family issues. Sometimes, though, we have to force ourselves to check in and reconnect with the Source's power, wisdom, and guidance.

You're the driver. It's up to you to put on the brakes and say, "I *am* listening and I *am* open. Please help and show me." If you really mean it and you're prepared to act upon the guidance that you're given, then anything is possible. Get out of the way, because just by asking, you're tapping into the power of your soul. Situations and opportunities in your life will shift and begin to manifest. The question is: Will you let them, or will you choose to stay where you are? I really feel that one of the things stopping you from being truly successful is a lack of belief in yourself.

In Chapter 1, I asked you to imagine yourself to be the automobile of your choice. The outside or frame of the car is your physical *body;* the driver is your *soul,* steering the vehicle in the direction of different destinations; and the gas that fuels the vehicle is your *spirit.* The Divine force of spirit is what animates and feeds your soul, pushing you ever forward to strive to be all that you are, all that you can be, and all that you could ever hope to be in this life. Therefore, checking in with yourself is a bit like a tune-up for the soul.

Checking in is a good way of reminding yourself that you're not just a soul; you're also a physical being. You have to honor and take care of yourself and your health. When you're developing your soul senses (that is, your intuition), it's important to have a fit body to help the mind and soul. The language of the soul is intuition. Your body acts like one huge psychic antenna operating at its own level of receptivity. Spiritual philosophies teach us that the universal life force runs through everything, including *you*. So at the risk of stating the obvious, make sure that you get plenty of rest, eat properly, and venture out in nature. This will promote a healthy body and remove the blocks that prevent intuition from flowing freely. The better the antenna, the clearer the reception!

Your soul will always lead you back to a place where it's safe. It's important to pay attention to your Soul Cry-Outs, taking the time to check in with your inner guidance on a regular basis to give yourself that tune-up. This is a great way to stay connected with the Source, the Divine force that fuels your soul. If you don't take a moment each day to listen, the link will get harder to reestablish every time. You owe it to your whole *self* to invest at least five minutes daily. If you're having difficulty finding or making that small amount of time, then I would implore you to take a good, hard look at how much you value *all* of you — body, mind, and soul.

EXERCISE: Soul Check-In

Intuition, which is filled with the universal energy that enhances your overall well-being, flows on the breath. For this exercise, just close your eyes and breathe deeply. Relax and let your awareness bring you back into your body. Follow your breath to the silent, still place within your heart. Inhale a few times into this area and continue to relax until you feel grounded. Your body and mind will begin to grow quieter with each breath.

Let your thoughts come in, just noticing them and watching them go out again. Imagine in your mind's eye that as you breathe in and out, pure universal energy is running up and down your spine. As this power flows through your body, it's clearing and spinning your energy centers (chakras), and your soul becomes infused with Source energy. Next, bring your awareness into your solar-plexus area, and ask your intuition and your soul if there's something that they want to tell you. Breathe and pause here for a moment, acknowledging whatever comes. As with so many of the exercises, I recommend that you keep your journal nearby so that you can record your thoughts as well as those soul flashes and intuitive messages.

This technique is also great if you have a decision that needs to be made. Get a Post-it note and stick the following affirmation on your computer or someplace where you'll see it clearly every day as a reminder to check in with your intuition and your soul before you hastily move forward:

I pause and ask before I act.

Touching Lives

Just as light shines through a prism and radiates a spectrum of beautiful, vibrant colors, so too do the people and incidents that touch your life on a daily basis. One of the most important lessons you'll learn at this time is how reaching out to others will help you renew your faith in yourself and humankind. You'll become more aware of the miracles that are all around you, including the ones that you had a hand in creating.

Through the work that I do, I've been blessed to get to meet so many different individuals from all over the world. People come into our lives for a reason. Some stay as we learn from each other, others go away forever, while a few keep coming back because there's a lesson to be completed. I met one special person who lives in Boston named Bren Bataclan. He may be just one man, but he's using his ability as an artist to touch many lives and hearts.

An article about Bren came across my desk while I was writing this book. He's a true living example of what I mean by leading a *soul-filled* life. In 1995, Bren moved to the East Coast from Ohio; and after living in Boston for a while, he noticed that this conservative, hectic, and busy city wasn't the same as the friendly, easygoing one that he'd been accustomed to back home. His story resonated with me on many levels. Earlier in this book, I talked about how we live in such a fast-paced world that we don't really take the time to notice and appreciate each other or the beauty around us.

Bren wanted to change that. He thought long and hard about how he could get people to just smile. He decided to resurrect the colorful cartoon characters that he'd painted as a child. You can't help but laugh and grin when you see these quirky figures. He initially left these small paintings all over Boston. When people would find them and see the characters looking up at them, they couldn't resist picking the paintings up and smiling. On the bottom of each one, Bren decided to attach a note with just a few words: "This painting is yours if you promise to smile at random people more often." That's all he wanted — nothing more, nothing less.

The thing I love the most about Bren's project is that through synchronicity I believe that people found these paintings at the exact time when they needed a little upliftment and joy in their lives. Maybe they decided to walk a different way home and came across one of Bren's characters smiling up at them from a park bench. Perhaps they might even have left it there, sensing that another person needed it more. Whatever the situation, I feel that they didn't just find the painting, but in truth, it found them. This wonderful story just goes to show you that on a soul level, everyone and everything in the Universe is connected — and one person can make a difference.

I know that you've felt this connection, this powerful force that's part of each and every one of us, although you may not have realized it. When you meet up with someone you haven't heard from in a long time, do you feel as though you're automatically drawn together as you embrace? Some people have this invisible pull. The same feeling can be experienced when it comes to nature, whether it's the woods, mountains, oceans, or one of the many other miracles that Mother Nature has blessed us with. This is the power of the Divine Source working through your soul — a force that you surely can't deny is there. This is the Source that continually reaches out through you to touch and affect as many lives as It can. It's part of your purpose of being all that you can be and living a life of ultimate passion.

Bren found *his* passion and purpose by making positive changes in the people around him. His paintings have now been given away in more than ten states across the U.S., as well as in other countries. He told me, "This is all about giving."

Bren decided to call his project "Smile Boston," and he continues to move people with his joyful art. For example, children in a Boston hospital can look up and find one of Bren's buddies looking back at them, making them giggle and turning the hospital environment into a less scary place. Bren is about to publish his own book, and once again people will undoubtedly be touched. I too can look up and see one of his works smiling back at me, reminding *me* to smile and not take life (and myself) so seriously . . . it goes by way too fast.

I've always been a connector — someone who brings people together with the foresight that they have a reason to meet. Even as a small child, I'd arrange for two people to get acquainted, *knowing* that doing so would benefit them. I continue this activity today, because I feel that as a soul, it's part of my purpose to assist others in any way I can. I move them to another level, and in this way, I help their souls evolve.

Hopefully, one day we'll all be able to do this for each other. Sometimes when I've orchestrated a meeting, people ask me, "What do you get out of it, John?" I want nothing in return, but I do receive real pleasure when the encounter results in a new opportunity or some other less tangible benefit. When it's my time to go to the Other Side, I feel that I'll cross over without the regret that I didn't try to do everything in my power to effect change.

Do you remember a time when a certain person came into your life and transformed your whole world or belief system? For all you know, that individual might have touched your life in a way that sent you in a completely new direction on your spiritual path. When people touch each other's lives, they may never realize the impact that a single interaction has on many other lives. Affecting someone else in a positive way is what being a spiritual being in human form is all about. It's about embracing life and living as a soul, learning, growing, loving, sharing, and constantly evolving during the time you have here. Helping others creates a ripple effect that will touch more people than you'll ever know.

I gave an elderly woman a hand the other day at the supermarket, and she looked at me as if she were in shock that someone actually took the time to help her. She told me that she'd had such an emotional day, and my assistance gave her the boost she needed. Maybe she passed on that positive attitude when she got home and someone else benefited. A simple act from an unexpected person, a stranger, and even children (who are truly our best teachers) can change our lives for the better. Such gestures nourish us with courage, hope, inspiration, and strength and oftentimes give us direction. By touching lives, we could quite possibly be creating miracles.

I know how hard it is at times to help others when you feel that you can't even help yourself, but it really does soothe your soul — try it. Since we're all unique, you'll touch another person's life in a way that may be totally different from how someone else would. You have to attach your own personal soul signature to it, just as Bren does when he gives away one of his paintings. You don't have to donate a work of art to affect lives, though . . . even a smile can move a mountain. Sometimes it might be as simple as a spontaneous kind gesture.

All I'm asking is that you be conscious of helping others. You may be saying, "But I'm just one person — what can I do?" You can't change the world overnight, but you *can* start by changing yourself. Whatever is going on internally will be reflected externally; if there's inner turmoil, then there will be outer confusion. Equally, when there's peace on the inside, it's likely that a life of calmness and serenity will follow on the outside. Everything in the world is based on the inner consciousness of humans. Always remember that one person (that means *you*) can make all the difference. You are a soul, so believe and know that you do have power and you *do* matter in this collective Universe.

EPILOGUE

As I draw to the end of my book, I contemplate what to
leave you, the reader, with. What can I impart to make one
more impression that will resonate with — and leave an imprint
on — your heart and soul?

I've grown to realize that as humans, we need to trust and
know that we never really go through this life alone. We're souls,
and as such, we'll always have God in our corner . . . the soul is
what keeps us linked to the one Divine Source. This part of us
brings a deeper understanding of life and the human connection
to a higher power.

I trust in the power of the soul and I really try to listen to its
wisdom, but I too am human and occasionally push it aside, imagining that it's just a thought from my own mind. Our soul is so
close and so tightly wrapped around our outer world that it may
be hard to distinguish its voice from that of our own ego. Just last
night, I heard my soul tell me to give a message to a couple I've
known for years but whom I hadn't spoken to for many months.
The information was so clear that I knew it wasn't coming from
my mind. As is so often the case, I wasn't even thinking about the
people it was intended for at the time.

The message was short and sweet: "Tell them God says hi!" I
had to trust that this clear-cut statement was exactly what I was
supposed to convey. Was it really from God? Who knows, but I was
sure that I could feel the energy of love behind the words, which is
usually my clue that the Divine Source is giving me inspiration to

pass on. I didn't know how important the message was until I called the couple. They were so surprised to hear from me as well as to get the message. They told me what they were going through right now — it was a time in their lives when big decisions were about to be made. They were asking themselves a bunch of questions: *Should we move? Should we buy a house? Will we have more financial security in the future? Can God hear us?*

Ironically, these two individuals are among the most spiritual and trusting people I've met in my life. They have faith in the power of spirit, their souls, and each other. I love what one of them told me: "John, we pray and trust in *Upper Management* that we'll be taken care of." I've never heard of God, the Divine Source, being called "Upper Management" before. How perfect!

The couple had been praying and asking for guidance, hoping for synchronicities to come into their lives and show them the signs to help them choose which direction to take. My phone call at that precise time with that unpretentious message was exactly what they needed to hear. They believe in the power of prayer, intuition, and meditation. They live their lives by connecting with each other on a soul-to-soul level and helping others by giving spiritual guidance and donating their time to charities. Most important, though, they don't just sit back and say, "Okay, Universe, bring it on!" Through the power of their souls, they meet the Source halfway. They value the fact that by turning inward to listen to their inner wisdom for clarity and direction and working on their *whole* self — body, mind, and soul — they'll lead a balanced and spiritually centered life.

As I said, I've known this couple for many years, and in some ways, their relationship parallels my own life. There are no coincidences. As I gave them that special message, I realized that it was as much for me as it was for them. As I finish this book, I want you to realize this acknowledgment from God is also meant for *you* right now at this precise time in your life. If you're faced with an important decision, you may very well need some guidance, too. If this is the case, then just trust that as a soul, you possess all the necessary resources to effect a positive outcome. Remember to pause and ask before you act — you'll be glad you did.

I wish you all the best on the chosen journey for your soul. It truly isn't the destination, but how you get there that's important. Always recall that as a soul, you have the power and choice to vibrate, shine, and illuminate. Follow the inner wisdom of your soul and you'll be on your way to a better understanding of who you are . . . and more important, who you can become.

RECOMMENDED RESOURCES

Books and Articles

Ask and It Is Given, by Esther and Jerry Hicks (Hay House, 2004)

Be Free Where You Are, by Thich Nhat Hanh (Parallax Press, 2002)

Creative Visualization, by Shakti Gawain (New World Library, 2002)

Discovering Your Soul's Purpose, by Mark Thurston (A.R.E. Press, 1984)

Excuse Me, Your LIFE Is Waiting, by Lynn Grabhorn (Hampton Roads Publishing Company, 2000)

Fast Food for the Soul, by Barbara Berger (New American Library, 2002)

Finding Your Answers Within, by Dick Sutphen (Pocket Books, 1989)

Getting to the Heart, by Athene Raefiel (Trafford Publishing, 2003)

Healers on Healing, edited by Richard Carlson, Ph.D., and Benjamin Shield (Jeremy P. Tarcher/Putnam, 1989)

Healing Mind, Body, Spirit, by M.J. Abadie (Adams Media, 1997)

The HeartMath Solution, by Doc Lew Childre and Howard Martin (HarperCollins Publishers, 2000)

"Journaling: Breathing space in the spiritual journey," by Jan Johnson (*Good News* magazine, November/December 2004)

Journey of a Soul, by John-Roger (Mandeville Press, 1975)

Just Say Om! by Soren Gordhamer (Adams Media, 2001)

"Love Your Life" (*Positive Thinking* magazine, May/June 2006)

The Magic of the Soul, by Patrick J. Harbula (Peak Publications, 2003)

The Magic of Psychic Power, by David J. Schwartz, Ph.D. (Parker Publishing, 1965)

Messages from the Masters, by Brian Weiss, M.D. (Warner Books, 2000)

The Power of Your Spirit, by Stephen O'Brien (Voices Books, 2003)

Real Prosperity, by Lynn A. Robinson (Andrews McNeel Publishing, 2004)

Science of Breath, by Yogi Ramacharaka (Yogi Publications Society, 1940)

Soul Love, by Sanaya Roman (H J Kramer, 1997)

Soul Power, by Nikki De Carteret (O Books, 2003)

Take Time for Your Life, by Cheryl Richardson (Broadway Books, 1999)

21 Steps to Reach Your Spirit, by Glyn Edwards and Santoshan (Quantum, 2001)

The Unmistakable Touch of Grace, by Cheryl Richardson (Free Press, 2005)

You Are the Answer, by Michael J. Tamura (Star of Peace Publishing, 2002)

Organizations

The following organizations are ones that I've worked with and that I both admire and recommend.

Al-Anon/Alateen
(888) 4AL-ANON
www.al-anon.alateen.org

Ancient Voices Harmonic Therapy
Didgeridoo Vibrational Medicine
(603) 433-7465
www.AncientVoicesHarmonicTherapy.com

The Arthur Findlay College (U.K.)
www.arthurfindlaycollege.org

Association for Research and Enlightenment
(757) 428-3588
www.edgarcayce.org

Bren Bataclan's Smile Boston Project
(617) 354-8040
www.bataclan.com

Celebrate Your Life! Conference
Mishka Productions
(480) 970-8543
www.MishkaProductions.com

Circles of Wisdom
(978) 474-8010
www.CirclesofWisdom.com

Friends Communities Website
www.FriendsCommunities.org

The Meta Arts Magazine
www.TheMetaArts.com

Movement of Spiritual Inner Awareness
www.MSIA.org

Ofspirit.com Weekly Magazine
(207) 967-9892
www.Ofspirit.com

Omega Institute
(845) 266-4444
www.eomega.org

Soul Purpose with Suzanne Falter-Barns
(518) 963-8927
www.HowMuchJoy.com/soulpurpose.html

Bereavement Information

Bereaved Parents of the USA
A nationwide organization designed to aid and support
bereaved parents and their families struggling to overcome
their grief after the passing of a child
www.bereavedparentsusa.org

The Compassionate Friends
A nationwide organization of bereaved parents offering friendship, support groups, and one-on-one assistance in your area
www.compassionatefriends.org

Wings
Information and inspiration for the bereaved and caregivers,
including a quarterly magazine of real stories about people's
journeys through grief
www.wingsgrief.org

Life-After-Death Information

After-Death Communication (ADC)
A comprehensive site produced by Bill and Judy Guggen-
heim, the authors of Hello From Heaven!
www.after-death.com

Afterlife 101
A site dedicated to providing knowledge about the afterlife
www.afterlife101.com

ACKNOWLEDGMENTS

Without a doubt, I am blessed with a phenomenal group of special friends and colleagues who support me, believe in me, and encourage and push me to be even more than I am . . . and above all, who respect and love me for just being me.

I want to express my appreciation to: Simon Steel, for his dedication and patience and for sculpting my words into works of art; D.Y.L.M.T.; and Debbie Eriksen, for 27 years of friendship and for helping me stay grounded. To the Steel family — I love you all, and you'll always be my second family. To Cheryl Richardson, a spiritual change agent for me — thanks for your friendship, guidance, and support. To Bob and Melissa Olson, who have been my constant supporters and friends; Vincent J. Barra, who keeps me connected to my routes, reinforces the path, and provides wise counsel; and Nancy Levin (Curly), who goes above and beyond — thank you for your friendship and the extra-special TLC. I would also like to thank Adrian, Mollie, and Christa — you truly make magic happen.

For their tireless and dedicated support behind the scenes, I want to thank my support team, Gretchen, Val, Craig, and Buck, who create the space in my life to allow me to concentrate on teaching, demonstrating, and writing. Your efforts never go unnoticed; you're helping heal and touch many lives. To **imageshaper. biz**, thank you for your incredible expertise in graphics and design. To my special Spirit Circle, Michael, Cheryl, Kerri and Missy, Bruce, and Max — thank you for sharing your souls. I love our special times together.

A special thank-you to Hay House and my fellow authors. I'm honored to be part of the extended family and to be involved in their purpose of enlightenment and positive change. To the team who runs Hay House Radio, thank you for helping put a little *soul* into the airwaves!

Thank you to the following for your friendship and support: Cathy Levine; Josh; Darlene; Kate and Yanick; Joyce; Renita and Brian; Jan (AZ); my new soul sister Colette Baron-Reid and Mark; Dimitri and Lorelei; Adrian Coros; Fran; Jordan Rich; Suzanne Northrop; Jenny Metevia; Mei-Mei; Josie and Des; Dottie, Louise, and Co. To Brian and Carole Weiss; Jess; and Pam B. — thank you for your continued support.

A special thank-you to Janis (JK), Rebecca, and Tom at CBS News Too Productions. We make a great team!

For all those who've shared their personal stories in this book, your stories are the ripple effect that reaches out to the hearts of thousands. Thank you to: Victoria and Quimby Nelson; Eric B.; Victor, Linda, and Bruce Dempster; Valerie; Bren Bataclan and the Smile Boston Project; Sister Aggie, wherever you are; Joe Carringer, for introducing me to the wonders of the didgeridoo; Aryaloka Buddhist Center; and so many others.

ABOUT THE AUTHOR

John Holland is an internationally renowned psychic medium and teacher who lectures, demonstrates, and reads for private clients; and who has spent more than 20 years developing his abilities. He has dedicated his life to personal development, which inspires him to teach others how to reconnect with their natural spiritual abilities with integrity and tap into their own unlimited resources.

John has been featured on The History Channel, A&E, *Unsolved Mysteries,* and in numerous articles; as well as becoming a familiar voice on radio stations throughout the world. He's the author of the bestsellers *Born Knowing* and *Psychic Navigator.*

For further information about John, his appearance calendar, and his workshop series; or to subscribe to his free e-mail newsletter, visit: **www.JohnHolland.com.**

NOTES

NOTES

NOTES

NOTES

⁘ ⁘ ⁘

We hope you enjoyed this Hay House book.
If you'd like to receive a free catalog featuring additional
Hay House books and products, or if you'd like information about the
Hay Foundation, please contact:

Hay House, Inc.
P.O. Box 5100
Carlsbad, CA 92018-5100

(760) 431-7695 or (800) 654-5126
(760) 431-6948 (fax) or (800) 650-5115 (fax)
www.hayhouse.com® • www.hayfoundation.org

⁘ ⁘ ⁘

Published and distributed in Australia by:
Hay House Australia Pty. Ltd., 18/36 Ralph St., Alexandria NSW 2015
Phone: 612-9669-4299 • *Fax:* 612-9669-4144 • www.hayhouse.com.au

Published and distributed in the United Kingdom by: Hay House UK, Ltd.,
292B Kensal Rd., London W10 5BE • *Phone:* 44-20-8962-1230
Fax: 44-20-8962-1239 • www.hayhouse.co.uk

Published and distributed in the Republic of South Africa by:
Hay House SA (Pty), Ltd., P.O. Box 990, Witkoppen 2068
Phone/Fax: 27-11-467-8904 • orders@psdprom.co.za • www.hayhouse.co.za

Published in India by: Hay House Publishers India,
Muskaan Complex, Plot No. 3, B-2, Vasant Kunj, New Delhi 110 070
Phone: 91-11-4176-1620 • *Fax:* 91-11-4176-1630 • www.hayhouseindia.co.in

Distributed in Canada by: Raincoast,
9050 Shaughnessy St., Vancouver, B.C. V6P 6E5
Phone: (604) 323-7100 • *Fax:* (604) 323-2600 • www.raincoast.com

⁘ ⁘ ⁘

Tune in to **HayHouseRadio.com**® for the best in inspirational
talk radio featuring top Hay House authors! And, sign up via the Hay House
USA Website to receive the Hay House online newsletter and stay informed
about what's going on with your favorite authors. You'll receive bimonthly
announcements about Discounts and Offers, Special Events,
Product Highlights, Free Excerpts, Giveaways, and more!
www.hayhouse.com®